A Man Without Equal

BILL BRIGHT

NewLife2000®
PUBLICATIONS
A Ministry of Campus Crusade for Christ

A Man Without Equal
Published by
NewLife2000 Publications
Arrowhead Springs 31-00
San Bernardino, CA 92414

Library of Congress Cataloging-in-Publication Data
Bright, Bill.
    A Man Without Equal / Bill Bright
        p.   cm.
    Includes bibliographical references.
    ISBN 1-56399-012-1 (pbk.)
    1. Jesus Christ—Person and offices.   I. Title.
BT202.B744   1992
232—dc 20

                                          91-28459
                                          CIP

Unless otherwise indicated, all Scripture references are from the *New International Version*, © 1973, 1978, 1984 by the International Bible Society. Published by Zondervan Bible Publishers, Grand Rapids, Michigan.

Scripture quotations designated NASB are from the *New American Standard Bible*, © 1960, 1962, 1963, 1968, 1971, 1972, 1973, 1975, 1977 by The Lockman Foundation.

Scripture quotations designated TLB are from *The Living Bible*, © 1971 by Tyndale House Publishers, Wheaton, Illinois.

Scripture quotations designated NKJ are from the *New King James* version, ©1979, 1980, 1982 by Thomas Nelson Inc., Publishers, Nashville, Tennessee.

Contents

Acknowledgments

Through the years, I have written many books and hundreds of articles. Almost forty years ago I wrote the *Uniqueness of Jesus*, which, in its written and recorded forms, was greatly used to introduce many people to Jesus. Now, I feel strongly impressed to expand and elaborate on that original material.

In the beginning years of my ministry, I personally researched, wrote, edited and polished each book manuscript and article.

Today, however, my responsibilities of leading a large worldwide movement and my appointments and travel schedule do not allow me such luxury.

In need of help, I happily sought the assistance of my good friend and Editorial Director, Don Tanner, and his staff to help me put into this book the essence of what I have taught for almost fifty years.

I have edited and polished this manuscript over and over again because I am so excited about the person and message of this book and its potential impact on millions of lives.

A special thanks to Don for his professional assistance in helping me prepare this manuscript. I also want to thank Joette Whims, Mary Taylor, Barbara Fagan, Greg Kriefall and Art McFarlane for their extensive help in assisting me in the development of this book and for joining Don and me in the editorial process.

1

What's All the Excitement?

The distinguished professor and dean of a famous theological seminary appeared to be in profound thought as we entered his cluttered study. Thousands of books filled the shelves that lined his office.

I was invited to visit this internationally known scholar by a friend who had been his student at the seminary.

My friend, the associate pastor of a historic local church, introduced me. "This is Bill Bright, president of Campus Crusade for Christ. He works with students and professors all over the world."

Politely waving us to sit down, the professor asked curiously, "Mr. Bright, when you talk to students about becoming a Christian, what do you tell them?"

Not wanting to appear shallow and simplistic to such a learned man, I weighed my words carefully. Before I could reply, the professor furrowed his brows and asked a second question: "Better still, what would you tell me? I would like to become a Christian."

Now I was really puzzled and even more cautious. Why would a world-famous scholar and theologian, the dean of one of the most prestigious seminaries in the world, ask a total stranger to help him "become a Christian?"

"Before you answer my question," he interjected, "let me give you the background of my spiritual quest."

With transparent honesty, he explained that his father was a famous scholar who denied the deity of Jesus of Nazareth. His father and his teachings profoundly influenced his own views—that Jesus was a great and good man, but not the Son of God.

"But my heart was never satisfied," he confessed. "I had no peace. Then a couple of years ago, I began my own research in earnest. I had to know the truth."

He paused thoughtfully, then related how he had studied the passages in the Bible concerning Jesus with new interest. He also had searched the writings and biographies of great Christian leaders of the centuries. "Now I am absolutely persuaded that Jesus is more than a great leader and teacher. He is the Son of God, the Savior of men!"

The professor told us that he believed this intellectually, but did not know Jesus as St. Augustine, Martin Luther, John Wesley and others knew Him. "I want to know Him personally as they did. Can you help me?"

My heart leaped for joy. Using a spare piece of paper on the professor's desk, I drew a circle on it. "This represents your life," I explained. In the circle I drew a throne, and on the throne I wrote the letter "S" for self. Pausing, I pointed to the "S."

"To become a Christian you must receive Christ as your Savior from sin. To live a full, abundant life, you must surrender the control of your life to Him by making Him your Lord and Master..."

We were interrupted by a knock on the door. It opened slightly, and a voice said, "Your next appointment is here, Professor."

At the professor's insistence, my friend and I returned two days later to continue our conversation. He greeted us warmly and took us into an office with no telephones.

Locking the door behind us, he spoke enthusiastically. "I went to church early this morning to take communion to prepare my heart for your coming. I have been waiting for you. Can you help me? I want to know Jesus as my personal Savior."

My pastor friend, quiet until now, spoke up skeptically. "Professor, are you sure you understand what you are saying? Do you truly believe that Jesus is the Son of God, the only Savior of men?"

The professor sighed, a bit impatient. "I have wrestled with these intellectual questions all of my life and have found no answers." Turning to me, he continued. "After several years of personal research, I am now absolutely convinced that Jesus is the Son of God. And I am fully persuaded that no honest person who is willing to consider the overwhelming evidence proving the deity of Jesus Christ can deny He is the Son of God. Now, will you pray for me?"

First I prayed; then he prayed; and my friend prayed. That day this man of international renown received Jesus Christ of Nazareth as his Savior by faith in the spirit of a little child. Later I was reminded of the words of Jesus: "Unless you turn to God from your sins and become as little children, you will never get into the Kingdom of Heaven" (Matthew 18:3, TLB).

It was a historic, life-changing experierience for this great man and an unforgettable day for my friend and me. The professor's whole life was transformed. His teachings and philosophy of life were revolutionized.

Every day more and more people are taking a look—and some, a second one—at the historical person of Jesus of Nazareth. Men and women everywhere are getting excited about Him.

My wife Vonette and I, along with thousands

of our associates, have personally observed this same hunger for Jesus in approximately two hundred countries around the world. On university campuses, in hundreds of metropolitan centers, in towns, villages and primitive or remote areas, we have witnessed this hunger for Jesus Christ.

This is strongly evidenced by the four hundred and sixty-five million people who have flocked to see the film "JESUS".* Wherever the film is shown, people of all walks of life gather to learn more about Jesus. Tens of millions have responded to the invitation to make Him their Savior and Lord.

Only recently we returned from the Soviet Union. For ten days we participated in three "JESUS" film premieres under prestigious sponsorship in Moscow, Leningrad and Kiev.**

---

* Figure as of 1991. The "JESUS" film was sponsored and financed by Campus Crusade for Christ, produced and directed by John Heyman, and distributed by Warner Brothers of Hollywood. This film is a fulfillment of a dream God gave me as a new believer in 1945. Thirty e years passed before it became a reality. In the first ten years after its completion, the film was viewed by nearly one-tenth of the world's population with tens of millions expressing a desire to follow Christ. By 1991, the film had been translated into more than two hundred major languages.

** See Appendix B.

In each case, we showed the film to top government officials—including mayors and ministers of education, justice and finance—as well as intellectuals and other leaders. Hundreds of actors, actresses, producers, directors, writers, and other dignitaries in the film makers' union also viewed the film and responded enthusiastically with many receiving Christ.

We also heard Kalevi Lehtinen, one of Europe's leading Christian spokesmen and one of our Campus Crusade for Christ staff evangelists, speak about Jesus to approximately 75,000 people. At three separate meetings in Leningrad, he spoke to audiences of more than 25,000, and an estimated seventy million viewed the final meeting on television. An estimated 50 to 80 percent of those hearing his messages at the meetings responded to his invitation to personally place their trust in Jesus Christ as Savior and Lord.

On Easter Sunday 1991, I preached on the resurrection of Jesus in the Palace of Congress behind the Kremlin walls. Again from 50 to 80 percent of the 5,000 people present responded to the invitation to receive Christ. The message was carried on nationwide television. According to officials, the broadcast reached a potential audience of 250 million viewers. It is believed that a minimum of 100 million viewed the program and that many millions received

Christ as their Savior via television on that day.

We have seen a similar response to Jesus of Nazareth around the world.

Perhaps you are wondering, *What's all the excitement? Why do His life and teachings still generate such interest today?*

Jesus is the most remarkable and fascinating person in history. He has inspired more hope, taught more compassion, and shown more love than any other man who has ever lived.

When He walked on earth, Jesus stirred people wherever He went. Crowds followed Him; hands reached out to Him; voices called to Him; people pushed and sometimes trampled one another[1] just to see Him, to hear Him teach, to bring their sick to be healed.

Jesus' popularity grew until many wanted to make Him king of the Jews. Once, when He entered Jerusalem, the capital city of Israel, crowds lining the wayside pulled off their cloaks and broke off palm branches to throw in front of Him. Voices shouted:

"Hosanna to the Son of David!"

"Blessed is he who comes in the name of the Lord!"

"Hosanna in the highest!"

When He entered Jerusalem, the whole city took notice. People gathered asking, "Who is this man?"

Others answered, "This is Jesus, the prophet from Nazareth" (Matthew 21:9-11).

What was there about this man that caused a stir wherever He went?

History's Greatest Revolutionary

Some time ago, a brilliant, young medical student from another land and a devout follower of an eastern religion came to see me. Through the months that I had known him, we had become good friends.

I asked this young man several questions. "Who in your opinion is the greatest leader that the world has ever known? Who has done the most good for mankind?"

After a moment of hesitation, he replied, "I am sure that Jesus has done more good than anyone who has ever lived. I would say that He is the greatest leader."

Then I asked, "Who do you think is the greatest teacher?"

No doubt he considered Socrates, Aristotle, Plato, Confucius and the other great philosophers of ancient and modern times. But he answered, "The greatest teacher is Jesus."

Finally, I asked, "In your opinion, who in the entire history of man has lived the most holy life?"

Immediately he answered, "There has never been anyone like Jesus."

I have posed these questions to men of all religions, as well as atheists and Communists. The answer from all knowledgeable people is always the same: "Jesus."

Indeed, there has never been anyone who could compare with Jesus of Nazareth. He is unique among all the human beings who have ever been born.

Philip Schaff, well-known historian and author of *The History of the Christian Church*, said:

> *Jesus of Nazareth, without money and arms, conquered more millions than Alexander, Caesar, Mohammed and Napoleon; without science and learning, He shed more light on things human and divine than all the philosophers and scholars combined; without the eloquence of the school, He spoke words of life such as were never spoken before, nor since, and produced effects which lie beyond the reach of orator or poet. Without writing a single line, He has set more pens in motion and furnished themes for more sermons, orations, discussions, works of art, learned volumes, and sweet songs of praise than the whole army of great men of ancient*

and modern times. Born in a manger and crucified as a malefactor, He now controls the destinies of the civilized world and rules a spiritual empire which embraces one-third of the inhabitants of the globe.[2]

Wherever the true message of Jesus Christ has gone, people and nations have been revolutionized, resulting in new life, new hope, and new purpose for living. Indeed, without fear of contradiction, we can regard Jesus Christ as history's greatest revolutionary. Everything about Him was unique: The prophecies of His coming. His birth. His life. His teachings. His miracles. His death. His resurrection. His influence on history and in the lives of hundreds of millions of people.

But many are uncertain about who Jesus was and why He came. Confused about the relevance of His teachings for them today, they question His place in their lives, or wonder, *Who is this Jesus? Why is He different from other men of history? What does He mean to me today? How can I know Him personally?*

To find answers to these important questions, we will explore several reasons Jesus is considered by knowledgeable people all over the world to be the greatest Man who ever lived:

1. The prophecies of His coming as the Messiah were precise and accurate.

2. The claims He made about Himself were extraordinary and unprecedented.

3. The birth of Jesus was unique.

4. His childhood was unparalleled.

5. His teachings were innovative and life-changing.

6. His death was sacrificial and necessary.

7. His resurrection was history's most revolutionary event.

8. His influence on people and nations through the centuries has changed the world.

Join me now in this exciting adventure to consider the unique life and ministry of Jesus.

2

"Who Do People Say
That I Am?"

Jesus' contemporaries were confused as to who He was. At times during His days on earth, even His disciples seemed unsure.

One day, Jesus led them away from the crowds to a deserted area.

Imagine the scene. Jesus leaves the disciples to go and pray alone.[3] Someone starts a campfire to warm the dusty-robed men while they wait for their Teacher to return. The crackling sounds of the fire help them to relax after a long, tiring day. They begin to talk about the miracles they have seen the Master perform: the dead raised,[4] the demon-possessed delivered,[5] the sick made well,[6] the feeding of the five thousand.[7]

One of His twelve disciples turns to the others. "I'll never forget the faces of those hungry people! And with only five small loaves and two fish, we fed them all! Wasn't it incredible how the bread and fish kept multiplying?"

Remembering the sight, the other men nod.

The first disciple looks down at his worn hands and continues. "I can't believe there was so much food left!"

"It was a miracle," someone else murmurs.

Another disciple quietly joins in, "I remember how the wind and the waves obeyed Jesus that stormy night on the lake..."

After a time, Jesus rejoins their little group. He lovingly looks at each of them, one-by-one. With a piercing gaze, He asks them a simple question, "Who do people say that I am?"[8]

The disciples pause at the intensity in His voice. What will they answer?

"Some of them think you are John the Baptist," they reply, "and others say you are Elijah or some other ancient prophet come back to life again."[9]

Was Jesus just a prophet? A teacher? A good man? Or was He much more than that?

For nearly two thousand years, ordinary people have considered these questions and expressed their views. Great political leaders, religious figures and scholars have all added their voices to the debate.

No Mere Man

Napoleon Bonaparte declared, "I know men; and I tell you that Jesus Christ is no mere man."[10]

Why would a man who conquered most of

Europe and who lived a life of ruthless ambition make such an astonishing statement?

Perhaps Napoleon's own failure made him think about his fate. After his defeat at Waterloo and during his exile on the Island of St. Helena, Napoleon had time to reflect on his life and to realize that death awaited even him.

To General Bertrand, a skeptic concerning the deity of Jesus and a faithful officer who had followed him into exile, Napoleon said, "Everything in Christ astonishes me. His spirit overawes me, and His will confounds me...He is truly a being by Himself. His ideas and sentiments, the truth which He announces, His manner of convincing, are not explained either by human organization or by the nature of things.

"Alexander, Caesar, Charlemagne, and myself founded empires. But on what did we rest the creations of our genius? Upon force. Jesus Christ alone founded his empire upon love; and, at this hour, millions of men would die for him."[11]

Many other leaders over the past nineteen centuries also have pondered the question, "Who is this Jesus?" Even during Jesus' day, rulers recognized that He was no ordinary person.

Jesus lived and ministered in an unstable political climate. Although Rome generally maintained the peace, political factions and the conditions in Palestine created tensions.

Pontius Pilate, a Roman prelate who held his office for ten years under the Emperor Tiberius, was a stubborn, arrogant man who took pains to provoke his Jewish subjects. When he first rode into Jerusalem, he raised Roman banners that he knew would offend the Jews.

Herod Antipas, tetrarch of Galilee and Peraea for about thirty years, and Pilate were enemies. Herod also was unpopular with many of the Jews because he ordered the beheading of John the Baptist.[12]

Understandably, the Jewish religious leaders chafed under Roman rule. The Pharisees* in particular were looking for the Messiah, a prophesied leader whom they believed would set up a political kingdom and allow the nation of Israel to dominate their oppressors. Consequently, the Pharisees heartily despised anyone who would dare suppress God's people.

Yet when Jesus, the "Man of Peace," came on the scene, these staunch political enemies united to crucify Him.

---

* The Pharisees were one of the three chief Jewish sects—the others being the Sadducees and the Essenes. The Pharisees were the strictest observers of the Law of Moses as well as Jewish religious traditions.

The jealous religious leaders, feeling threatened by the truth of Jesus' teachings and His integrity, plotted to kill Him. But how could they accomplish the deed? They had no political power to execute anyone.

The chief priests and elders conspired to arrest Jesus by night so that the people wouldn't riot. They bribed Judas, one of Jesus' twelve disciples, to betray Him by leading soldiers to the garden of Gethsemane where Jesus had gone to pray.

The fully-armed soldiers marched Jesus to the High Priest's house where the religious leaders branded Jesus a blasphemer for claiming to be equal with God and condemned Him to death.[13]

His accusers took Him to Pilate. In an effort to compel the Roman governor to carry out their sentence, they falsely charged Jesus with inciting the people to riot and with trying to set up His own kingdom.

Not wanting to deal with the difficult situation, Pilate sent Jesus to Herod. Herod, after ridiculing and mocking Jesus, sent Him back to Pilate. And the religious leaders followed, constantly accusing Him.

The Bible records Pilate's response:

You brought this man to me as one

who incites the people to rebellion, and behold, having examined Him before you, I have found no guilt in this man regarding the charges which you make against Him.

No, nor has Herod, for he sent Him back to us; and behold, nothing deserving death has been done by Him (Luke 23:14-16, NASB).

Attempting to pacify the demands of the accusers, Pilate offered to flog Jesus, then release Him. But the religious leaders wouldn't back down.

"Crucify Him! Crucify Him!" they demanded.

Pilate capitulated. Washing his hands to signify he wasn't responsible for shedding innocent blood, he turned Jesus over to the executioners.

Ever since Jesus' encounters with Pilate and Herod, the question "Who is this Jesus?" has been the topic of controversy among political leaders. Some have rejected Him and severely persecuted His followers. Many others, however, have shown through what they've said or done that they acknowledged His claims of deity.

Emperor Constantine began his rule as a worshiper of the Persian sun-god Mithra.

Tradition tells us that on the eve of a decisive battle, he saw a cross above the sun as it was setting. The cross bore the words, "In this sign conquer." He immediately painted Christian emblems on his soldiers' shields.

The next day Constantine's army defeated its enemies at the Milvian Bridge. As a result, he identified with Christ and became the first Christian emperor in history.

Throughout the years, many rulers followed in the footsteps of Constantine. For example, Clovis, the king of the Franks, converted to Christianity. In 800 Charlemagne knelt at St. Peter's Church in Rome while the pope placed the imperial crown on his head. And Otto I, king of Germany, came to the rescue of the church which was battered by warring feudal lords.

In the early 1600's, King James I commissioned the translation of an English Bible.

And Queen Victoria, who reigned over England during most of the 19th century, regularly visited the elderly and poor in the slums of London because of her faith in Jesus.

Most of the Founding Fathers and historic figures of the United States of America believed deeply in calling upon God to help them rule the affairs of the new nation. Some of them also spoke out about the person of Jesus.

●Patrick Henry, 18th century orator and Revolutionary leader:

I wish I could leave you my most cherished possession—my faith in Jesus Christ. For with Him you have everything; without Him you have nothing at all.

●Daniel Webster, 19th century orator and influential congressional leader:

I believe Jesus Christ to be the Son of God. The miracles which he wrought establish in my mind his personal authority, and render it proper for me to believe whatever he asserts... And I believe there is no other way of salvation than through the merits of his atonement.[14]

Modern political leaders have described the change that comes through Christ's work in the heart.

●Dr. Charles Malik, internationally-known statesman, professor of philosophy, and president of the General Assembly of the United Nations in 1959:

Only those who stay close to Jesus Christ can help others who are far away. Only those who prefer Him to everything else, even to the call of the needy world,

*can be used of Him for the need of the
world...The heart of the whole matter is
faith in Jesus Christ.*[15]

●James Baker III, U.S. Secretary of State
under President George Bush:

*Of course, power brings excitement
and invitations to some of the most
exclusive gatherings in the world...But
power does not bring inner security and
fulfillment. That comes only by developing
a personal relationship with God, which
for me is personified by Jesus Christ.
Inner security and real fulfillment comes
by faith—not by wielding power in the
town where power is king.*[16]

Without question, the life and message of
Jesus Christ has greatly influenced the course
of governments and the destinies of nations.
Remove Jesus from the palaces of the world,
and the history of the nations would be a
completely different story.

Simply a Prophet?

Remember the incident when Jesus asked
His disciples, "Who do people say that I am?"
(Mark 8:27, NASB).

The disciples' responses reflected popular
belief about Jesus. For example:

●The Samaritan woman at the well was astounded when Jesus knew all about her life. She said, "I can see that you are a prophet" (John 4:19).

●After Jesus raised the widow's son from the dead, onlookers were filled with awe and praised God saying, "A great prophet has appeared among us" (Luke 7:16).

●After hearing Jesus preach, some of the people said, "Surely this man is the Prophet" (John 7:40).

During his lifetime, Jesus gave many startling and accurate prophecies. Here are just a few:

1. He predicted that Judas would betray him (John 6:64,70,71).
2. He foretold His own death and resurrection (Luke 9:22).
3. He predicted the destruction of the temple in Jerusalem (Matthew 24:1,2).
4. He prophesied persecution for his followers in the days ahead (Matthew 10:16-18).
5. Jesus also foresaw world conditions in our present age—such as wars, rumors of wars, earthquakes, and widespread famine (Matthew 24-25).

Who would dare describe these future events in such detail?

Was Jesus simply a prophet? Or was He much more?

The lives and words of past and present religious leaders strongly support their belief in the divinity of Christ.

● Justin Martyr, an early church historian and philosopher who died for his faith in A.D. 166:

> But if you are willing to listen to an account of Him, how we have not been deceived, and shall not cease to confess Him—although men's reproaches be heaped upon us, although the most terrible tyrant compel us to deny Him—I shall prove to you as you stand here that we have not believed empty fables, or words without foundation.[17]

● John F. Walvoord, former president of Dallas Theological Seminary:

> The doctrine of the eternity of the Son of God is the most important doctrine of Christology as a whole because if Christ is not eternal then He is a creature who came into existence in time and lacks the quality of eternity and infinity which characterizes God Himself.[18]

● Dr. Walter Martin, the late founder of the Christian Research Institute:

> *There is, therefore, only one God by nature, one God who is omnipotent, omniscient, omnipresent, one God who possesses characteristics and attributes that may be imitated but never duplicated in finite creations. When it is said, then, that man is or can be "a god," we must remember that only He, the incarnate Word [Jesus], has the right to the title of deity among men, since He alone is designated "the only begotten God." [19]*

Without exception, what men have believed about Jesus of Nazareth—a prophet who was only a man or the God/Man who was the Great Prophet—has set the course of their lives and determined their destiny.

An Educated Guess

Many see Jesus as the greatest teacher in history. No other man has been quoted as often or has inspired as many books and articles. His teachings have given us clear, profound insights into the deepest questions of life.

Though little is recorded of His childhood, what is known of His early years suggests that He had a unique and deep understanding of the heart of God. The Bible records, "Everyone who heard him was amazed at his understanding and his answers" (Luke 2:47).

Those who heard Him speak as an adult were equally stirred. During the three years of His ministry, Jesus traveled throughout what today is the nation of Israel, teaching in the synagogues and healing the sick. Large crowds followed Him everywhere.[20] And Jesus' disciples left everything to walk with and learn from Him.

What kind of a teacher could inspire such loyalty?

First, *He was compassionate*. Jesus cared about those around Him. God's holy Word says, "When Jesus landed and saw a large crowd, he had compassion on them, because they were like sheep without a shepherd. So he began teaching them many things" (Mark 6:34).

He had a deep love for the hurting and needy. He healed diseases and raised the dead; He visited the sinners and encouraged the outcasts. In fact, His teaching and His compassionate deeds were inseparable.

Second, *He was innovative*. Jesus used stories and parables to illustrate spiritual truths.

Two of His most popular parables are "The Good Samaritan" and "The Prodigal Son." He also used familiar objects such as sheep, grape vines, farming and marriage customs to help His listeners understand abstract truths.

He taught through His own example as well. During His last meal before His crucifixion, He wrapped a towel around His waist and, going from one of His disciples to the other, knelt to wash their feet.

When He finished, He asked, "Do you understand what I have done for you? You call me 'Teacher' and 'Lord,' and rightly so, for that is what I am. Now that I, your Lord and Teacher, have washed your feet, you also should wash one another's feet. I have set you an example that you should do as I have done for you" (John 13:12-15).

Third, *He spoke the truth regardless of the consequences.* Jesus never changed His message to avoid a scene or to pacify His listeners. In speaking the truth lovingly but bluntly and honestly, He made many enemies—especially among the teachers and religious leaders of Jerusalem.

Because Jesus frequently spoke against the hypocrisy of the scribes and chief priests, they nursed a bitter hatred for Him and eventually succeeded in having Him crucified.

Fourth, *He spoke with revolutionary wisdom and authority.* Jesus said things that people had never thought of or spoken before. He declared that His words and wisdom were not His own, but had come directly from His Father, God.[21]

A discourse full of profound truths, His "Sermon on the Mount" reinforces this claim. The Bible records, "When Jesus had finished saying these things, the crowds were amazed at his teaching because he taught as one who had authority, and not as their teachers of the law" (Matthew 7:28,29).

Without question, the greatest teaching of Jesus was that salvation comes, not by what man does for God, but by what God does for man through His Son.[22]

This teaching of salvation by faith in Jesus as God's Messiah, not works, was unique and revolutionary because ritualistic Judaism and other religions taught that man could reach God or paradise through his good deeds. Jesus repeatedly emphasized good works, but never as the means to salvation.[23]

One day, a group of people approached Jesus and asked, "What must we do to do the works God requires?" Jesus replied, "The work of God is this: to believe in the one he has sent" (John 6:28,29).

Fifth, *His teaching changed lives.* Nicodemus was one of the Pharisees, a group of religious leaders who hated Jesus and plotted to destroy Him. When Nicodemus sought out the Master Teacher late one night, Jesus explained the necessity of spiritual birth to enter the Kingdom of God. His words, "You must be born again" (John 3:7, TLB), had a tremendous effect on Nicodemus' life.

Jesus' impact on Nicodemus is clearly evident in subsequest events related to Jesus' arrest and crucifixion. When the chief priests and other Pharisees searched for ways to arrest Jesus, Nicodemus tried to intercede. "Does our law condemn a man without first hearing him to find out what he is doing?" (John 7:50,51). But his words fell on deaf ears.

Then, after the crucifixion, he accompanied Joseph of Arimathea, a member of the Sanhedrin, to ask Pilate for the body of Jesus. After getting permission to bury the body, Nicodemus took seventy-five pounds of spices and helped wrap His remains for a kingly burial.[24]

Down through the centuries, the lives of hundreds of millions around the world have been changed by His teachings. Many have reaffirmed the declaration of those who heard him speak, "No man ever spoke like this Man" (John 7:46).

Almost everyone would admit that Jesus of Nazareth was a great teacher. Even His enemies had to acknowledge His timeless wisdom. But was He more than a teacher? Great scholars have expressed their ideas, affirming the Person of Christ and His influence on their lives:

• Josephus, Jewish historian of the 1st century:

> *About this time there lived Jesus, a wise man, if indeed one ought to call him a man. For he was one who wrought surprising feats and was a teacher of such people as accept the truth gladly.*[25]

• Erasmus, 15th and 16th century Dutch scholar, theologian and writer:

> *The sum of all Christian philosophy amounts to this:—to place all our hopes in God alone, who by his free grace, without any merit of our own, gives us every thing through Jesus Christ.*[26]

• Blaise Pascal, 17th century French mathematician, scientist and philosopher:

> *Jesus Christ is the center of all, and the goal to which all tends.*[27]

• Feodor Dostoyevsky, 19th century Russian novelist:

> *Even those who have renounced Christianity and attack it, in their inmost being still follow the Christian ideal, for hitherto neither their subtlety nor the ardor of their hearts has been able to create*

a higher ideal of man and of virtue than the ideal given by Christ of old.[28]

●Lew Wallace, 19th century lawyer, U.S. General, and author:

After six years given to the impartial investigation of Christianity, as to its truth or falsity, I have come to the deliberate conclusion that Jesus Christ was the Messiah of the Jews, the Saviour of the world, and my personal Saviour.[29]

Some scholars who believed that Jesus was just a man later reversed their thinking out of intellectual honesty and became followers of Jesus.

I was deeply moved while reading about one such scholar in the magazine section of the *Los Angeles Times* early one Sunday morning in about 1949. My eye fell on a picture of a venerable old professor, Dr. Cyril E.M. Joad, and the dramatic story of the change that had taken place in his life.

One of the world's greatest philosophers, Dr. Joad was for years head of the Philosophy Department at the University of London. He and his colleagues—Julian Huxley, Bertrand Russell, H.G. Wells and George Bernard Shaw—had probably done more to undermine the faith of the collegiate world of the last generation than any other group.

Dr. Joad believed that Jesus was only a man and that God was a part of the universe. Should the universe be destroyed, he taught, God would also be destroyed. He believed that there is no such thing as sin and that man was destined for utopia.

The article described the many years he had been antagonistic toward Christianity and how he denied the existence of sin. However, he said that two world wars and the imminence of another had conclusively demonstrated to him that man was indeed sinful. Now he believed that the only explanation for sin was found in the Bible and that the only solution for sin was the cross of Jesus Christ. Before his death, Dr. Joad became a zealous follower of Christ. I have in my library one of his last books entitled *The Recovery of Belief.*

Consider too the example of C.S. Lewis. A writer and professor at Oxford and Cambridge Universities in England, he was an agnostic for years. He tried to convince himself that Christianity was invalid. But after a long process of searching for answers, he received Christ as his own Savior and Lord while he was at Oxford. He describes that moment:

> *You must picture me alone in that room in Magdalen, night after night,*

feeling, whenever my mind lifted for even a second from my work, the steady, unrelenting approach of Him whom I so earnestly desired not to meet. That which I greatly feared had at last come upon me. In the Trinity Term of 1929 I gave in, and admitted that God was God, and knelt and prayed: perhaps, that night, the most dejected and reluctant convert in all England.[30]

C.S. Lewis became a devout follower of Jesus and wrote many books advocating his belief in Christ. In *Mere Christianity,* he writes, "You can shut Him up for a fool, you can spit at Him and kill Him as a demon; or you can fall at His feet and call Him Lord and God. But let us not come up with any patronizing nonsense about His being a great human teacher. He has not left that open to us. He did not intend to."[31] C.S. Lewis concluded that Jesus is indeed more than a good, moral teacher—He is the Savior of the world.

In the coming pages, we will examine the amazing facts concerning the life and ministry of Jesus Christ. We will learn what the Old and New Testaments of the Bible have recorded about His nature. And we will discover the astounding claims He has made about Himself.

But this isn't an expedition into dusty, yellowed old books or boring, academic theologies. Rather, it's a thrilling adventure of meeting the One who has changed the world, who has taught the most eminent scholars, who has directed the course of powerful nations and inspired billions of men and women to follow Him. It is a journey into the life and mind of the most revolutionary Person in history.

3

The Center of Prophecy

The Old Testament, written by many individuals over a period of 1,500 years, records a myriad of astounding predictions. For example, the prophets made detailed forecasts of the rise and fall of nations, the spiritual highs and lows of the nation of Israel, and a future time of terrible calamity and tribulation. Many of these predictions have already been accurately fulfilled. Other events are still in the future.

Not only does the Bible announce what lies ahead, it also sets strict criteria for the prophets who gave the predictions. In the Old Testament, God said to Moses:

> *I will raise up for them a prophet like you from among their brothers; I will put my words in his mouth, and he will tell them everything I command him. If anyone does not listen to my words that the prophet speaks in my name, I myself will call him to account. But a prophet who presumes to speak in my name anything I have not*

commanded him to say, or a prophet who speaks in the name of other gods, must be put to death.

You may say to yourselves, "How can we know when a message has not been spoken by the Lord?" If what a prophet proclaims in the name of the Lord does not take place or come true, that is a message the Lord has not spoken. That prophet has spoken presumptuously. Do not be afraid of him (Deuteronomy 18:18-22).

The most amazing Old Testament prophecies are those promising a Jewish Messiah. They mystified scholars for thousands of years. Not understanding how to fit the prophecies into a single picture, the scholars viewed them as pieces of a giant puzzle. The details seemed to contradict or to make little sense. Devout Jews, however, trusted that God would reveal His timely solution.

More than three hundred separate references to the coming of the Messiah included many unique details. The Old Testament prophet Micah, for instance, described the precise location of the Messiah's birth: "As for you, Bethlehem Ephrathah, little as you are among the thousands of Judah, from you shall He come forth to Me, who is to be ruler over Israel. His goings forth are from old, from days of eternity" (Micah 5:2, Berkeley).

This small village is the very place where Jesus Christ was born. Is this prophecy a lucky coincidence, or is there certainty that this man Jesus fulfilled every detail predicted of the coming Messiah?

PROPHECIES OF JESUS' BIRTH		
Old Testament Prophecies	Details of Prophecies	Fulfillment in Jesus
Genesis 12:1-3	Descendant of Abraham	Matthew 1:1 Luke 3:34 Matthew 1:2
Genesis 49:10	Descent through the tribe of Judah	Luke 3:33
Micah 5:2	Birth in Bethlehem	Luke 2:4,5,7
Daniel 9:25	Time for His birth	Luke 2:1,2
Isaiah 7:14	Virgin birth	Luke 1:26,31
Isaiah 9:7	Heir to the throne	Luke 1:32,33
Jeremiah 31:15	Slaughter of children	Matthew 2:16-18
Hosea 11:1	Flight to Egypt	Matthew 2:14,15

Space does not allow a complete analysis of prophecies concerning Christ and their fulfillment. But the eight prophecies listed in the chart are typical of the accuracy of all Old Testament predictions.

Now let us apply three standards of accuracy to these prophecies.

First, *could these predictions have occurred by chance?*

Peter W. Stoner, a professor of mathematics and astronomy, explains the probabilities of eight prophecies being fulfilled in one person. "We find that the chance that any man might have lived down to the present time and fulfilled all eight prophecies is 1 in 10^{17} of being absolute [in mathematical terms, 10^{17} = one hundred quadrillion or 100,000,000,000,000,000]."

To describe how remote a possibility this number represents, Stoner suggests that, after laying one hundred quadrillion silver dollars two feet deep across the state of Texas, we mark one of them and stir the whole mass of them thoroughly. We blindfold one man and ask him to pick up one silver dollar from anywhere in Texas, but he must pick up the marked coin. The probability of his retrieving the exact one is the same likelihood that the prophets had of writing these eight prophecies in their human understanding and of having them all come true, in any one man, from their day to today.

"Now these prophecies were either given by inspiration of God," says Stoner, "or the

prophets just wrote them as they thought they
should be. In such case the prophets had just
one chance in 10^{17} of having them come true
in any man, but they all came true in Christ."[32]

And that is not even considering the odds
against the other hundreds of prophecies that
Jesus fulfilled in detail!

Second, *could Jesus have manipulated
events to make it seem as if He fulfilled these
predictions?*

No ordinary person has ever selected the
time, place or family into which he was born.
Only someone with supernatural power could
choose the timing of His birth. How could an
ordinary man have engineered the census that
brought His parents, Mary and Joseph, to
Bethlehem while Jesus was still in His mother's
womb? Or have foreseen the flight of His
family into Egypt when He was only two years
old? Or have fulfilled the many other prophecies of His later life and death?

Third, *could Jesus have guessed the out-
come of the seemingly contradictory prophecies of the coming Messiah?*

No historian or any other person could
have predicted the manner in which Jesus
would come into this world. The fact that the
Messiah is connected with two distinct places—
Bethlehem and Egypt—and is called neh-zer,

meaning the "Nazarene," is too conflicting, yet precisely correct, to be simply a guess.[33] The mystery was not solved until Jesus was actually born and fulfilled these prophecies.

Neither could anyone have guessed the precise details concerning His death unless he were more than a man. During the crucifixion, for instance, the soldiers cast lots for His clothing as King David, one of the most powerful and godly kings of ancient Israel, predicted.[34] We could take other prophecies of the coming Messiah and apply these standards as well. For example:

- The names He would be given (Isaiah 9:6)

- His Galilean ministry (Isaiah 9:1,2)

- His rejection by His own people (Isaiah 53:3)

- His triumphal entry into Jerusalem (Zechariah 9:9)

- His betrayal by a close friend (Psalm 41:9)

- His crucifixion between thieves (Isaiah 53:12)

- His burial with the rich (Isaiah 53:9)

- His resurrection and ascension (Psalm 16:10; 68:18)

In each case, not one detail failed to come to pass. Every point of every prophecy concerning Jesus met God's standard for accuracy. No other person in history can claim to have met this requirement. Christ fulfilled 100 percent of all the Old Testament predictions of the birth, life, death and resurrection of the Messiah!

The New Testament makes an even more revolutionary claim—that Jesus Christ is the center of all biblical prophecy. The Scripture proclaims:

> *God, Who gave to our forefathers many different glimpses of the truth in the words of the prophets, has now, at the end of the present age, given us the Truth in the Son (Hebrews 1:1,2, Phillips).*

And the Book of Ephesians declares:

> *God has allowed us to know the secret of His Plan, and it is this: He purposes in His sovereign will that all human history shall be consummated in Christ, that everything that exists in Heaven or earth shall find its perfection and fulfillment in Him (Ephesians 1:9, Phillips).*

The evidence is overwhelming. The precise fulfillment of the immense body of biblical prophecy is found in one unique and revolutionary Man—Jesus of Nazareth. Claiming that He was the predicted One of old, Jesus stepped into time. And the pieces of the prophetic puzzle slipped into place.

So far, we have discovered what political figures, religious leaders and scholars have said about Jesus. We have also seen how He fulfilled the Old Testament prophecies of the coming Messiah. Now let us look at the claims that Jesus made about Himself.

4

In His Own Words

One Sabbath the usual crowd gathered in the synagogue at Nazareth. Somber scribes, prestigious religious leaders and devout laymen patiently waited to hear the Word of God read aloud.

The synagogue attendant brought out a sacred old scroll containing a part of the Bible written hundreds of years before by the prophet Isaiah. Jesus, the carpenter's Son, was chosen to read.

The Spirit of the Lord is upon me,
because he has anointed me
to preach good news to the poor.
He has sent me to proclaim freedom for the
prisoners
and recovery of sight for the blind,
to release the oppressed,
to proclaim the year of the Lord's favor
(Luke 4:18,19).

Then He rolled up the scroll and handed it back to the attendant. Every eye watched as He sat down. Confidently, He looked around and announced, "Today this scripture is fulfilled in your hearing" (Luke 4:21).

What kind of man would dare to announce that He was God's Sent One, the Promised Messiah? How could He prove this outrageous claim?

Revolutionary Claims

Jesus of Nazareth made many startling statements about Himself:

He declared He was God: "I and My Father are one...He who has seen Me has seen the Father" (John 10:30; 14:9, NASB).

He professed to be the only way to God: "I am the way, the truth and the life. No one comes to the Father, except through Me" (John 14:6, NKJ).

He affirmed that His words were eternal: "Heaven and earth will pass away, but My words will never pass away" (Mark 13:31).

And He asserted divine authority: "All authority in heaven and on earth has been given to me" (Matthew 28:18).

But these are only a few of the many radical claims He made about Himself. Let us consider some of the others:

Jesus said He was:	Scripture reference:
Able to forgive sins	Mark 2:5; Luke 7: 48-50 John 8:24
The Son of Man	Matthew 8:20; 11:19; 26:2; Luke 7: 34; 9:58
The Judge of the world	Matthew 7:21-23
The fulfillment of Scripture	Luke 24:44
The Bread of life	John 6:35
The Light of the world	John 8:12
The "I Am"	John 8:54-59; 18:5,6
Divine	Matthew 4:7; 12:6-8; Mark 14: 61-64
Able to save the lost	Luke 19:10; John 10:9; 11:25
Eternal	John 8:58; 17:5
Sinless	John 8:46; 14:30
Able to accomplish God's work	John 17:4

Could a man who has without question accomplished more good for the human race than anyone who has ever lived be deluded about Himself? What man could make these seemingly presumptuous claims unless He truly was God in the flesh? If Jesus is who He claimed to be, how can we know for sure?

Making Sure

Jesus' character and ministry and the witness of those who knew Him best offer abundant evidence to support His radical claims of deity.

The testimony of His character: The Gospels record the life of Jesus. From the beginning, He exhibited gracious and godly qualities unequalled then or since. He demonstrated amazing wisdom, and His understanding and knowledge astounded His followers and dumbfounded His enemies.[35]

His bearing was always under control, and He never failed to please God.[36] As we have observed, Jesus' compassion was endless—even with the crowds that flocked to touch Him and to be healed.[37] He was humble and meek; not even His enemies could accuse Him of pride or pretentiousness. He was patient with all who welcomed Him, did not prefer the rich or famous, and treated children with love and tenderness.[38] Jesus spent many hours praying for those who would follow Him and preparing Himself for the suffering that He knew lay ahead on the cross.[39] In all ways, His character was pure and selfless.

Jesus was also sinless. When in the desert, He resisted temptation through the power of God's Word. Throughout His life and ministry,

He was totally obedient and faithful to God. Nowhere do the Gospels record one instance in which He yielded to sin. One New Testament writer testifies of Jesus, "We do not have a high priest who is unable to sympathize with our weakness, but we have one who has been tempted in every way, just as we are—yet was without sin" (Hebrews 4:15).

Jesus also proved His divine character through His immeasurable love, a passion never equalled in history. Knowing the depths of human depravity, He nevertheless willingly offered Himself as a sacrifice to pay for every sin and evil committed by the rebellious human beings He had created. He endured the wrath of His Father toward sin to heal and restore each person who would accept His free gift of everlasting life.[40] Only God in the flesh could so unselfishly love such unlovely creatures!

The proof of His ministry: Jesus proclaimed that He was indeed the Son of God. Consider these proofs:

1. He fulfilled Old Testament Scriptures concerning His birth, life, death and resurrection (Isaiah 7:14; Zechariah 9:9; Isaiah 9:1,2; 53:3-12; Psalm 16:10).

2. The wisdom of His teachings and His

authoritative understanding of God's holy Word astounded all who heard Him (Matthew 7:28,29; 22:15-46).

3. He worked miracles of healing, cast out demons, commanded the seas and weather and performed other extra-ordinary acts (Mark 1:34-42; 4:37-41; John 11:39-45).

4. He quietly and matter-of-factly received worship and devotion from His follow-ers and from the crowds (Matthew 14:33; John 9:38,39; 12:13).

5. He publicly pardoned sin (Matthew 9:28).

6. He predicted future events, including His own death and resurrection and the destruction of the temple at Jerusalem (Matthew 23:37-24:2; Mark 8:31).

7. He gave power to His followers and sent them out to cast out demons and heal the sick (Matthew 10:1).

8. He perfectly obeyed God's commands, even to the point of crucifixion (Luke 22:42; 23:44-48).

9. He displayed divine power through His resurrection and ascension (John 20; Acts 1:1-12).

Every miracle Jesus performed, every sermon He preached, every lesson He taught further proved that He was who He claimed to be, the Son of God, equal with God the Father.

The witness of His followers: Jesus drew many responses from people who heard His claims. Some worshipped Him as did the crowd during His triumphal entry into Jerusalem. A leper whom Jesus healed fell at His feet.[41] So did the man who was born blind.[42] His disciples worshipped Him.[43] Many people who saw Him day after day were convinced He was more than a man.[44]

The events following His death also prove that Jesus was the Messiah. Before His death, for example, the disciples were timid, frightened men. They deserted Him when He was arrested, cowered during His trial, and stood at a distance when He was crucified.

Yet later, these same men, convinced of His resurrection and filled with the Holy Spirit, revolutionized the world with His teachings. They and other believers endured hardship and persecution, and many were martyred for their Savior and Lord.

The testimonies of some of His closest followers are recorded in the New Testament. Peter begins one of his epistles, "Simon Peter, a servant and apostle of Jesus Christ, to those who through the righteousness of our *God and Savior, Jesus Christ* have received a faith as precious as ours" (2 Peter 1:1). John, the beloved disciple of Jesus, says of Him, "No man has seen God at any time; the only begotten God, who is in the bosom of the Father, He has explained Him" (John 1:18). Stephen, the first martyr for Christ, called upon his Savior as he was being stoned, "*Lord Jesus,* receive my spirit" (Acts 7:59, KJV). And Paul writes, "Looking for the blessed hope and glorious appearing of our *great God and our Savior Jesus Christ*" (Titus 2:13, NKJ). These and other New Testament Christians proved through their transformed lives that Jesus Christ is truly the only One who can change the human heart.

Through the centuries, hundreds of millions have found the reality of Jesus' claims to be true in their lives.

For almost fifty years, it has been my personal privilege to have worked with and introduced many thousands of students, professors, and other adults in all walks of life to Jesus Christ. Thousands have shared with me their profound gratitude for the way Jesus has changed their lives and expressed their eternal thanks for all that He has done and is doing for them. Certainly, this is one of the greatest proofs that Jesus is everything He claimed to be.

But before we can completely answer the question, "Who is this Jesus?", we must also examine His mission and how He fulfilled it.

5

Unique Among Men

Man has long searched for the Creator of life and the answers to his age-old questions: "Who am I?" "Why am I here?" "Where did I come from?" "Where am I going?"

Let us return to our beginning.

I can just imagine it. The moment of man's creation. From the ground God scoops fresh earth, molding it carefully into a marvelous new form. The body lies before its Sculptor ready for life. With a smile of satisfaction, the Maker bends low and breathes deeply into the still figure. The breath of life fills the lungs.

A wave of warmth surges through the body, infusing it with strength.

The figure speaks slowly, "Who am I?"

His Maker smiles. "You are man, and your name is Adam. I have made you this day as the crown of My creatures."

"Why am I here?" Adam rises to his feet.

"To fellowship with Me and bring glory to My name!" the Holy One replies.

56

"What is my future?"

"I will create from your rib a companion, and you shall be man and wife. Your destiny is to multiply yourselves, fill the earth with your kind, and have dominion over all that I have made."

The Sculptor peers admiringly at His creation. The pleasure of God echoes throughout the heavens in triumph, "It is very good."[45] So began the journey of man.

Destiny Turns to Disaster

God created man with a free will—the power to choose his own destiny—and put within him the principle and power of obedience. With the knowledge of God's will, Adam knew the rewards of obedience and the penalty for disobedience. But would he obey?

As a test, God placed a tree in the Garden of Eden. Eating of its fruit would destroy Adam's innocence and enable him to know good and evil, which would result in his death and the fall of the human race. "From the tree of the knowledge of good and evil you shall not eat," God warned, "for in the day that you eat from it you shall surely die" (Genesis 2:16,17, NASB).

I'm sure you've heard the familiar story—

how the serpent, Satan,* beguiled Eve, who then ate of the forbidden fruit and gave it to her husband. Adam knew the consequences of his act but chose to eat the fruit anyway. His act of disobedience caused "the Fall" of mankind from innocence and separated humanity from the loving Creator.[46]

The consequences were devastating.

First, *the Fall sabotaged God's plan for man* by usurping the authority that belongs to God and violating man's dependence upon Him. As man became independent of his Creator, his eternal tie with God was broken.

Second, *pain, hardship, and sorrow came.* The woman suffered in child-bearing. For the man, the ground was cursed and no longer yielded good fruit without cultivation. Thorns and thistles overran the land. As a result, exhausting physical labor became his lot. Driven from the Garden of God, humanity faced an unknown future in a cursed and desolate world.[47]

Third, *death—separation from God—condemned man to eternal, spiritual darkness* and consigned him to Satan's kingdom. In the

---

* Satan is pre-eminently "the Adversary." He is hostile to all goodness and is the chief opponent of God and man. He aims to undo the work of God and seeks to persuade men to sin.

process, fear of God replaced fellowship with God, and shame over sin obscured the joy of innocence.[48]

Mankind in this moment of self-will lost the seed of eternal life. Now, instead of living forever, his days were numbered; his destiny ruined. The writer of the Old Testament book of Ecclesiastes poignantly describes this disaster.

> *This only have I found: God made mankind upright, but men have gone in search of many schemes. This is the evil in everything that happens under the sun: The same destiny overtakes all. The hearts of men...are full of evil and there is madness in their hearts while they live, and afterward they join the dead (Ecclesiastes 7:29; 9:3).*

In their disobedience, Adam and Eve followed a crafty old pied piper, Satan, into a tunnel of disbelief and deceit. Emerging from the other end, they and all humanity after them had to face the tragic result of their waywardness. They could no longer view their destiny clearly. The results of their defiance are visible everywhere—dysfunction, disease, decay and death.

The question is often asked of me, "Why should billions of people suffer because of the sin and disobedience of one man, Adam?" Because he was the representative of mankind down through the ages. Let me explain.

In modern history, we have seen the rise of many ruthless dictators such as Adolph Hitler, Joseph Stalin, the Ayatollah Khomeini and Saddam Hussein. The decisions these men made affected the lives of every citizen of their countries. The deeds of these ungodly leaders caused injury and death to many millions of men, women and children.

Similarly, Adam's sin produced death and decay for those he represents. Every man and woman born on this earth has suffered for Adam's willful disobedience. Thus the writer of Ecclesiastes observes, "Death is the destiny of every man; the living should take this to heart" (Ecclesiastes 7:2).

Why Jesus Came

The transgression of our first parents was a voluntary elevation of the will of man over the will of God. It was a deliberate trespass of a divinely marked boundary, a decision to exchange the word of the living God for the lie of His depraved enemy. Each human being born since has inherited this tendency to go his own way. It is called the sin nature.

Man's self-will is characterized by an attitude of active rebellion or passive indifference. Because of sin, he is by nature degenerate and corrupt. With his understanding darkened and conscience defiled, his thoughts and affections are worldly, sensual and "full of evil."

In this condition, man is destitute of God's love, undeserving of His forgiveness, filled with hostility to all that is godly, possessed of a nature that is constantly on the downgrade, and in bondage to a dominion from which he cannot free himself.[49]

With man in such a state, how could he ever be reunited with his Creator? How could he be restored to fellowship and fulfill his intended destiny? Man needed to be redeemed. But who could be his redeemer?

God had a wonderful plan. Not an afterthought of the Fall, it was a glorious preplanned work which He conceived before the creation of man.[50] The plan involved God's unconditional love and perfect justice.

Imagine getting a traffic ticket for speeding. When you show up in court, your own father is the judge. Would it be fair for him to fine everyone else who has a ticket, but excuse you because you are his child? Of course not.

Suppose, then, he fines you one hundred dollars. Since you do not have the money, you must spend thirty days in jail. But because he loves you, your father steps down from the judge's bench and pays the fine for you. Justice is satisfied; you go free. The only condition is that you accept your father's payment.

Similarly, man could not redeem himself. Only one who was without sin could satisfy the justice of God. The substitute had to be a man to take the place of man. He had to be sinless to die for the sinner. Since humanity could not provide such a redeemer, that savior had to come from God.

To this purpose, God in the person of His only begotten Son, Jesus Christ, conceived by the Holy Spirit and born of a virgin, offered Himself as the required substitute. Coming to this world and taking man's place, He accepted the full penalty for man's sin.[51] Because He was man, He could die, and because He was God, He could die for the sins of the whole world.

Jesus Came With a Sense of Mission

Jesus said to Zacchaeus, the corrupt tax collector, "Today salvation has come to this house... for the Son of Man has come to seek and to save that which was lost" (Luke 19:9,10, NKJ). One cannot read the New Testament accounts of the life of Christ without realizing that this was His mission.

From His earliest youth and throughout

His life, Jesus knew He was a man of destiny. The Bible shows us how clearly He understood His mission and purpose.

First, *as a boy of twelve, He claimed to be doing God's will.* He had come with his parents to Jerusalem to celebrate the Feast of the Passover, a Jewish holy festival. When they left for home, He lingered behind and was not missed by them until the next day. Joseph and Mary found Him several days later sitting among the amazed scholars, "both listening to them and asking them questions" (Luke 2:46).

When asked why He had stayed behind, Jesus was surprised—as though His parents should have known. "Why is it that you sought Me? Did you not know that I must be about My Father's business?" (Luke 2:41-49, NKJ).

Second, *God proclaimed Jesus His beloved Son.* When Jesus was baptized by the prophet John the Baptist in the River Jordan, the heavens opened to Him, "and He saw the Spirit of God descending like a dove and alighting upon Him. And suddenly a voice came from heaven, saying, 'This is My beloved Son, in whom I am well pleased'" (Matthew 3:13-17, NKJ).

Third, *Jesus' selection of His disciples demonstrated an awareness of His Messianic mission.* When He called Nathanael to be His disciple,

Jesus said, "You will even see heaven open and the angels of God coming back and forth to me, the Messiah" (John 1:51, TLB).

Fourth, *Jesus acknowledged His eternal glory*. He prayed, "Father, the hour has come...I have glorified You on the earth. I have finished the work which You have given Me to do. And now, O Father, glorify Me together with Yourself, with the glory which I had with You before the world was" (John 17:1-5, NKJ). Here we see Jesus approaching His finest hour with the knowledge of His eternal existence and destiny.

How He Fulfilled His Mission

With such a great task before Him, how did Christ carry out His mission? The story begins with a young virgin in Nazareth. The New Testament records this startling event:

> *God sent the angel Gabriel to Nazareth, a village in Galilee, to a virgin, Mary, engaged to be married to a man named Joseph...*
>
> *Gabriel appeared to her and said, "Congratulations, favored lady! The Lord is with you!"*
>
> *Confused and disturbed, Mary tried to think what the angel could mean.*

"Don't be frightened, Mary," the
angel told her, *"for God has decided to
wonderfully bless you! Very soon now,
you will become pregnant and have a baby
boy, and you are to name him 'Jesus.' He
shall be very great and shall be called the
Son of God..."*

*Mary asked the angel, "But how can
I have a baby? I am a virgin."*

*The angel replied, "The Holy Spirit
shall come upon you, and the power of
God shall overshadow you; so the baby
born to you will be utterly holy—the Son
of God..."*

*Mary said, "I am the Lord's servant,
and I am willing to do whatever he wants.
May everything you said come true."
And then the angel disappeared (Luke
1:26-38, TLB).*

Christ's virgin birth simply means that,
"contrary to the course of nature, Jesus was
divinely conceived by the Holy Spirit in the
womb of Mary. In such a conception, deity
andhumanity were fused together and Jesus
came forth as the God-Man."[52] The whole
superstructure of the Christian faith depends
upon this fact.

Had Jesus been born of a mortal man as well as a mortal woman, He would not have been sinless nor the only Son of God as He claimed, but a mere man with no power to forgive sin. In turn, we would have been deprived of His unique character, and we would have been separated from God, lost in our sins forever, and denied our eternal destiny.

Because of His virgin birth, Jesus has a dual nature: He is both the Son of God and the Son of Man. Our finite minds cannot begin to comprehend what that means, but it is true. In this "hypostatic" or personal union of the human and divine natures in Christ, the eternal Son of God took upon Himself a complete, but sinless, human nature and became Man.[53] As the Son of God, His mission was to go to the cross and pay the penalty for our sins, which no human being could accomplish. As the Son of Man, His purpose was to identify with all aspects of our humanity. And because of His unique nature, Jesus could do so without sin.[54]

Christ's dual nature is vital to God's plan of deliverance. Finis Jennings Dake in his commentary, *God's Plan for Man*, writes:

> *It was not only important that He have two natures, human and divine, for the sake of man, but also for the sake of*

*God, to be a true mediator between God
and man...As God He can uphold the
dignity of Deity, and as man He can be
truly sympathetic and meet the needs of
man.*[55]

Jesus alone is able to bridge the gulf between the holiness of God and the sinfulness of man. Only through Him do we find the way to God and experience His love and forgiveness and the assurance of eternal life.

Our Lord is unique not only in His revolutionary birth and nature, but in how He lived and in what He taught as well. As the Son of Man, Jesus is the ideal of what God wants us to become.

In His absolute submission to God the Father, in His full surrender to God's Holy Spirit, in His unquestioning obedience to the will of God, in His total triumph over temptation, in His sinless life and miraculous ministry, in His purposeful prayers, Jesus is our supreme example.

At the heart of these marvelous qualities is Christ's matchless and infinite love. Unlike the Hollywood image of love which is based on lust and selfishness, Christ's love is selfless, unconditional, and sacrificial. This sacrificial love cost Jesus His life.

With two thousand years of advances in

education, technology, philosophy and science, we have never produced another who is worthy to be compared with Jesus. His divinity and humanity are without parallel among men.

But the ultimate expression of His revolutionary life was His death. Jesus Christ was the only man in all of history who was born to die. His death had a four-fold purpose:

1. To pay the penalty of our sin and rescue us from the sentence of death.

2. To provide the basis on which God could set forth His righteousness and yet pardon sinful man.

3. To liberate us from Satan's kingdom.

4. To reconcile all who would repent of their sins to God.

Paul brings this purpose into focus in one of his letters:

> *It was through what His Son did that God cleared a path for everything to come to him—all things in heaven and on earth—for Christ's death on the cross has made peace with God for all by his blood...and now as a result Christ has brought you into the very presence of God, and you are standing there before him with nothing left against you...the only*

condition is that you fully believe the Truth, standing in it steadfast and firm, strong in the Lord, convinced of the Good News that Jesus died for you, and never shifting from trusting him to save you (Colossians 1:20-23, TLB).

Hundreds of millions of people around the world have discovered this marvelous path. The Bible records that God has liberated us "out of the darkness and gloom of Satan's kingdom and brought us into the kingdom of his dear Son, who bought our freedom with his blood and forgave us all our sins" (Colossians 1:13,14, TLB). If you have trusted Jesus Christ as your Savior and Lord, you too are a living testimony of this truth.

Jesus' death was only part of the redemptive process. Without His resurrection and ascension, His sacrifice would have been incomplete, and we would have remained under the penalty of death. The resurrection, as we shall see, is the final proof that Jesus Christ is who He claimed to be. And His ascension into heaven signified the completion of His mission on earth as the Savior who made possible man's restoration to his original destiny.

6

Resurrection Revolutionary

The validity of Jesus' claims about Himself rests on the resurrection—whether He rose from the dead or stayed in the grave.

During my ministry which began in 1945, I have met many skeptics of the resurrection, both students and laymen alike. Some have said that to believe in a risen Christ is nothing more than a blind leap of faith with little or no basis in truth. When confronted with the facts, however, those who were intellectually honest have been forced to admit that the resurrection is a historical event based on irrefutable proofs.

On my spiritual journey from agnosticism to a vital, living faith in Christ, I too had a problem with the resurrection. How could a human being who had died be raised from the dead? I was willing to believe, but not at the risk of losing my intellectual integrity. So I began to investigate the evidence.

Evidences of the Resurrection

My personal study brought me to a firm

conviction that a bodily resurrection is the only explanation for Christ's empty tomb. Five evidences helped me reach this conclusion.

First, *Christ predicted His resurrection.* The Bible records, "From that time Jesus Christ began to show His disciples that He must go to Jerusalem, and suffer many things...and be killed, and be raised up on the third day" (Matthew 16:21, NASB). Even though His followers did not understand what He was telling them at the time, they remembered His words and recorded them. Matthew, Mark, and Luke each describe the predictions in their accounts of Christ's life.

Second, *Jesus made numerous appearances to His followers.* On at least ten occasions after His death, Jesus appeared to those who had known Him. In each instance, He related to them as the living, loving Savior. He comforted the mourners outside His tomb on Sunday morning.[56] On the road to Emmaus, He explained things about Himself from the Old Testament.[57] Later, He ate in their presence and invited them to touch Him. Scripture records that Jesus was seen by more than five hundred at one time.[58] Each time, His friends were assured that He was alive and in bodily form.

Some may argue that a few people could have agreed to a deception, but how can one explain the collaboration of five hundred people? History convinces me that these witnesses actually saw Jesus with their own eyes following His resurrection.

Third, *the unrelenting faith of the disciples* convinces me of the resurrection. Those disciples who were once so afraid that they deserted their Lord now courageously proclaimed this news, risking their lives to preach the facts of the resurrection of Jesus. Most of them died as martyrs proclaiming Jesus' death and resurrection. Their bold and courageous behavior does not make sense unless they knew with absolute certainty that Jesus had been raised from the dead.

Fourth, *the growth of the Christian church* confirms the resurrection. Peter's first sermon, which dealt with Christ's resurrection, stirred people to receive Him as their living Savior. Luke records the thrilling results: "There were added that day about three thousand souls" (Acts 2:41, NASB). And that group of believers has multiplied until now it reaches around the world. Today, there are hundreds of millions of believers—more than ever in history. Surely, without a powerful, resurrected, living Founder, the Christian church would never have been born or would have slowly faded and eventually died.

Finally, *the testimony of hundreds of millions of transformed lives through the centuries* shows the power of the resurrection. Second Corinthians 5:17 gives glorious assurance that everyone who truly receives Jesus Christ into their lives will be forever changed. Countless numbers who have accepted Jesus Christ as their Savior and Lord give evidence of His resurrection power to break the bonds of sin and produce righteousness and peace in their lives. Many have been delivered from addictions. The destitute and despairing have found hope. Broken marriages have been restored. Sufferers have been comforted. The most conclusive proof for the resurrection of Jesus Christ is that He is living within believers today in all of His resurrected life and transforming power.

Indeed, the resurrection sets Christianity apart from all the religions of the world. No religion can claim that its founder was raised from the dead and that he lives today in the hearts of His followers. No other religious leader has broken the power of death and conquered sin. Only Christianity is based on the historical evidence of a risen Christ and an empty tomb.

Significance of the Resurrection

The resurrection confirms that Jesus is who He claimed to be. Let us consider the magnitude of this event.

The resurrection proved that Christ was divine. The fact that Jesus Christ died on the cross in itself does not prove He is God. Many have died on a cross. Jesus proved His deity by fulfilling the prophecies of His death and by His return from the grave. The Bible declares that "by being raised from the dead... [Christ] proved to be the mighty Son of God, with the holy nature of God himself" (Romans 1:4, TLB).

The resurrection proved Christ's power to forgive sin. If Jesus had not been raised from the dead, His claim to be the Savior of mankind would be empty. His death would be reduced to that of an ordinary man.

The Bible asserts, "If Christ has not been raised, your faith is futile; you are still in your sins" (1 Corinthians 15:17). But by rising from the dead, Jesus proved His authority and power to break the bonds of sin and to assure forgiveness and eternal life to all who accept His gift of salvation.

The resurrection revealed Christ's power over death. The Bible records, "Christ rose from the dead and will never die again. Death no longer has any power over him" (Romans 6:9, TLB). The resurrection secured our victory over death as well and "lifted us up from the grave into glory along with Christ, where we sit with him in the heavenly realms" (Ephesians 2:6).

The resurrection defeated God's enemy. One cannot begin to fathom the depth of enmity between Satan and God. From the moment of his original rebellion until the day of the cross, the devil fought viciously and cunningly to overthrow the kingdom of God. He spoiled God's greatest creation in the Garden of Eden, and having ruined man, he struggled fiendishly to thwart the coming of the Savior who would restore mankind to its original destiny.

Satan must have thought he had dealt the final and decisive blow in this age-old war when Jesus went to the cross. By killing the Son of God, he had ruined God's plan for redemption. But this was the devil's most serious miscalculation. The cross was *heaven's* triumph. And when Jesus Christ arose, the power of sin and death was forever shattered.

Christ's conquest is also the believer's victory. Because of the resurrection, Christians need never fear Satan or death again.

Completing His Mission

As He faced His own death, Jesus began preparing His followers to carry on His work. He had taught that there are two commandments. The first is to "'Love the Lord your God with all your heart and with all your soul and with all your mind and with all your strength.'

The second is this: 'Love your neighbor as yourself'" (Mark 12:30,31).

For forty days after His death and resurrection, Christ appeared many times to His followers. On one occasion, He gathered His remaining eleven disciples on a mountain in Galilee and gave them His "Great Commission." He said, "Go and make disciples of all nations, baptizing them in the name of the Father and of the Son and of the Holy Spirit, and teaching them to obey everything I have commanded you. And surely I am with you always" (Matthew 28:19,20). His instructions were a revolutionary strategy for fulfilling the two commandments He had given by proclaiming the Good News of God's love and forgiveness to the world. Later, on the Mount of Olives, He admonished His disciples to wait in Jerusalem until they were filled with the Holy Spirit and then to take His message to Jerusalem, Judea, Samaria and to the ends of the world.[59]

Immediately after, He rose skyward and disappeared into the clouds, leaving the disciples staring after Him in amazed wonder.

The ascension of Christ was the final act in the drama of redemption. His mission completed, Jesus Christ was exalted to His former glory. The Gospel of John records the prayer Jesus prayed just before He died:

> *Father, the time has come. Glorify your Son, that your Son may glorify you. For you granted him authority over all people that he might give eternal life to all those you have given him. Now this is eternal life: that they may know you, the only true God, and Jesus Christ, whom you have sent. I have brought you glory on earth by completing the work you gave me to do. And now, Father, glorify me in your presence with the glory I had with you before the world began (John 17:1-5).*

From His glorified position in heaven, Jesus now intercedes before God on our behalf as our High Priest. Formerly, a high priest offered sacrifices for the sins of the people. In completing the redemptive process, Jesus took upon Himself this high priestly role. The New Testament explains, "Because Jesus lives forever, he has a permanent priesthood. Therefore he is able to save completely those who come to God through him, because he always lives to intercede for them" (Hebrews 7:24,25).

The resurrection of Jesus Christ ranks as history's most revolutionary event. One cannot deny that He shook the world in His day. But His life just as dramatically has shaped the course of history to our time.

7

He Changed the World

No other person in history has influenced the world for good more than Jesus Christ. His life and message have greatly changed the lives of people and nations. History is His Story. Remove Jesus of Nazareth from history, and it would be a completely different story.

For the past 2,000 years, He has been the centerpiece of humanity. Charles Spurgeon, an English theologian, wrote:

> *Christ is the great central fact in the world's history. To him everything looks forward or backward. All the lines of history converge upon him. All the great purposes of God culminate in him. The greatest and most momentous fact which the history of the world records is the fact of his birth.*[60]

Consider today's date on your calendar. It gives witness to the fact that Jesus of Nazareth, the Christ, lived on the earth. B.C. means before Christ; A.D., anno Domini, is the Latin phrase translated, "in the year of our Lord."

Believers who spread Christianity demonstrated an active, transforming energy and pure integrity that affected every society they touched. Samuel Zwemer, a professor of missions at Princeton Theological Seminary in the early 1900's, said:

> *The gospel not only converts the individual, but it changes society. On every mission field, from the days of William Carey, the missionaries carried a real, social gospel. They established standards of hygiene and purity, promoted industry, elevated womanhood, restrained antisocial customs, abolished cannibalism, human sacrifice and cruelty, organized famine relief, checked tribal wars, and changed the social structure of society.*

It would be impossible to show the magnitude of Christ's influence on the world. I can only help you step closer to the mural of history to examine a few of the ways in which His life and message have made a dramatic difference in civilization.

Social Reform

Jesus fed the hungry, healed the sick, comforted the bereaved and loved the outcast.

Believers through the centuries have followed His example. The more serious the social problems, the greater the desire of Christian men and women to find remedies for these ills.

From the beginning, the followers of Jesus treated individuals with a dignity and worth unknown to their pagan culture. As a result, wherever missionaries took the true gospel of Christ, social conditions dramatically improved and cultures were enriched.

Early Christians, for example, helped soften the harshness of Roman slavery and contributed to its decline. They taught reverence for womanhood, which was unknown in Roman society, and stressed the permanence and sacredness of marriage.

During the Middle Ages, the church provided an alternate to marriage for women by fostering religious careers. Many devout women became important spiritual and civic leaders.

The Reformation stirred both Roman Catholics and Protestants toward one of the greatest movements of social reform in history. Among other changes, Christians moved for prison reform and built orphanages. And the growing numbers of married clergy gave increased honor to the wife and family.

In the 19th century, religious revivals stirred devout men and women to push for new social reforms. Efforts included the formation of groups to combat alcohol abuse, to fight for the abolition of slavery, and to give women the right to vote. It was the clergy who set up the first agencies to provide social services.

Zealous missionaries established orphanages, provided famine relief, raised the status of women and worked to abolish cruel social customs, including cannibalism and human sacrifice. Other Christian leaders, such as William Booth, who founded the Salvation Army, began endeavors to relieve human suffering in urban areas.

Today, committed Christian believers are fighting to eliminate abortion and halt euthanasia; they are working diligently to reduce child abuse, drug addiction and alcoholism; they are seeking to eliminate pornography. Christian organizations are coordinating actions against age-old problems such as prejudice, poverty, famine and family dysfunction. Christian organizations are coordinating actions against age-old problems such as prejudice, poverty, famine and family dysfunction.

Medicine

Jesus Christ also felt concern for those who suffered from disease and handicaps. He cured the leper, healed the lame, and gave sight to the blind. In the process, He taught His disciples to show the same compassion.

Believers have cared for the sick ever since the time of Christ. By the Medieval period, the church was establishing hospices and hospitals. And during the 18th and 19th centuries, hospitals became centers for medical training and research as well as for healing. New institutions, such as the Red Cross, were mostly the work of individual believers and Christian denominations or churches. These organizations arose to care for the mentally ill, encourage public health education, and relieve human suffering.

Although much of Western society, inspired by Christian example, now provides health care through secular sources, the medical work of missions continues in many parts of the world. For multitudes of disadvantaged people, medical supplies, immunizations, and surgical and hospice care come from missionaries and native Christians who bring the love of Christ in word and deed.

Business

The principles Jesus taught have made an impact on the world of business. The early church taught the dignity of labor, and believers were admonished to work hard and to shun laziness. During the Middle Ages, monasteries improved agriculture by developing crop yield and methods of tillage. The church also insisted on a just price for goods and fair wages for the worker.

The Reformation inspired dramatic changes in the world of business. By emphasizing every vocation as a "call" from God, Christians encouraged the growth of a new urban middle class. This new spirit of commerce stimulated navigational exploration and the settlement of unknown lands.

The turbulence of industrialization, urbanization and immigration in the 18th and 19th centuries brought hardship and poverty to millions of people across Europe and North America. Under the leadership of John Wesley and George Whitefield, many Christians, individually and in groups, began striving for reform in the workplace. Some fought for regulations to protect women and children in mines and industry. Others opposed forced labor, helped enact child labor laws, and formed labor unions.

In the 20th century, many godly men such as J.L. Kraft of Kraft Cheese and J.C. Penney, who founded a merchandizing empire by that name, built businesses based on biblical principles. They funneled large percentages of their profits into the church or worthy social projects. They sought to make work conditions fair and profitable for their employees and gave of their personal wealth and time to spread the gospel of Christ.

Science

Christianity has had a profound influence upon science as well. The biblical view of an orderly and dependable universe formed and held together by a divine Creator became the foundation for many of history's scientific discoveries. Christ's teaching inspired the thinking of many celebrated forerunners of modern science, including Roger Bacon, Nicolaus Copernicus, Johannes Kepler, Galileo, Blaise Pascal, and Isaac Newton. Christian thought also was foundational to applied science—fostering industrialization, medical progress, space research, and advances in other scientific fields.

During the 19th and 20th centuries, however, many scientists have tried to separate science and religion, falsely asserting that natural processes prove God does not exist. Unable to prove or disprove the existence of God, they conveniently overlook the evidential order of the universe that early scientists looked for because of their belief in God.

But recent discoveries and developments show the emptiness of science without Christ. The problems of ecological imbalances stemming from scientific progress, the waste of resources, the ability to tamper with human genes, the ethics of test tube fertilization, and of nuclear and chemical weapons, point to the possible abuses of science divorced from God's design and standards. Today, an increasing number of scientists are joining a long list of famous forerunners who embraced a biblical faith in Christ.

Law and Government

Christian principles have had a significant effect on law and government. The early Christians promoted justice. Converted politicians worked for legislation on behalf of widows, orphans, and the poor and against immoral and harsh practices. Christ's influence strengthened resistance to barbaric invasions and brought orderly living to pagan tribes.

The foundation for much of today's international law came during the Middle Ages through Papal arbitration and from clerical bans on wars between neighboring princes. Christian convictions eliminated many of the crude methods of determining justice held over from the pagan past. Eventually, the state became the guardian of righteousness and peace throughout Europe.*

Nonconformist denominations planted the seeds of democracy. Many Reformation bodies were "gathered" churches. They gave every man a voice in their congregational govern-ments. Protestant groups eventually called for separation of church and state.

English common law was developed from the idea that man is accountable to a higher law based on the Bible. Similarly, biblical principles of freedom and justice provided a basis for the Constitution of the United States.

Christianity influenced many great statesmen. The first President of the United States, George Washington, began and ended each day on his knees in prayer and often quoted the Bible in his speeches and writings. President Abraham Lincoln regularly sought the counsel of God in making major decisions.

---

* The Pope, head of the Roman Catholic Church, used his religious authority to help encourage and negotiate peaceful relations among kings and kingdoms. His political authority at this time in history often superseded that of the kings.

In the middle 1950's, President Dwight D. Eisenhower helped give significance to the newly legalized National Day of Prayer for Americans.* He believed he was called of God to give leadership to spiritual renewal in the United States.

In many countries, especially much of the continent of Africa, mission schools educated a large proportion of the national leadership. Jomo Kenyatta, the first president of Kenya, attended school at the Church of Scotland mission in Kikuyu. He served three terms. Much of Kenya's post-independence political stability can be attributed to Kenyatta's wise leadership.

In Zambia Kenneth David Kaunda received his early training at the Lubwe Mission School. He later became a missionary for the Livingstone Mission, a spokesman for black Africans, and the President of his country. His Christian beliefs influenced his ideology for the development of Zambia. He was also

---

* My wife, Vonette, while chairman of the National Day of Prayer, lobbied both houses of Congress to declare the first Thursday of every May as the official National Day of Prayer. The vote was unanimous and signed into law by President Ronald Reagan. She also worked with both Presidents Reagan and George Bush who have called for a return to prayer and Bible reading in the schools.

considered by many as one of Africa's most honorable statesmen.

Arts and Culture

Christian ideals are reflected in art and culture. The early Christians redirected the pagan focus of the arts where they lived. Beginning with the New Testament, believers created a vast new literature in a dying Roman civilization. By the 6th century, the arts were preserved and developed almost exclusively within the church.

During the Medieval period, culture revolved around the cathedral. Mosaics, sculpture, paintings, stained glass, even new forms of architecture, were displayed in the house of God. Music, drama, art, and much of the literature centered around Christian themes.

As the Protestant movement expanded and enhanced the message of the church, artists were inspired by many different Christian schools of thought. Lutheranism introduced a new hymnody; Roman Catholicism influenced Rembrandt. DaVinci, Michelangelo and Raphael expressed their art and sculpture with epic biblical themes. The dynamic spiritual music of Bach, Beethoven and Handel rings down through the ages. John Bunyan, Dante and Milton centered their literature around scriptural motifs. Even artists who claimed no allegiance to Jesus Christ used Christian symbols and imagery in their work.

Education

One of the most consistent and important influences of Jesus Christ lies in education. In the first centuries, the church took upon itself the task of increasing literacy so that every believer could read the words of Jesus.

During the Dark Ages, the church alone maintained schools, founded universities which became the seats of intellectual activity, and developed great libraries. Eventually the Reformation brought learning to the masses, and literacy spread among women. A reconstruction of educational methods and curriculum resulted. Hundreds of Christian colleges were established—many of which are listed today among the most prestigious institutions in the world.

Wherever Christian missionaries settled, a rise in literacy followed. These devout believers gave written form to hundreds of languages and taught millions of people to read and write. Today, many mission groups continue their work in disadvantaged areas of the world.

The influence of Jesus is still revolutionizing our world. Christianity has spanned cultural diversities, prejudice barriers and political differences.

Truly Jesus Christ is the only answer to our world's needs today and in the future. Charles Malik writes:

> *I really do not know what will remain of civilization and history if the accumulated influence of Christ, both direct and indirect, is eradicated from literature, art, practical dealings, moral standards and creativeness in the different activities of mind and spirit.*

Indeed, how dark our world will be if men and women fail to let Jesus rule their hearts and nations. But how gloriously history will unfold when Jesus Christ is Lord of all!

So far we have seen how the unique birth, life, teachings, death, resurrection and exaltation of Jesus prepared the way for our restoration to God and to our eternal destiny. But one final step remains—one which only you and I can take.

8

"Who Do You Say I Am?"

Picture again with me the occasion when Jesus took His disciples away from the crowds to a deserted area where He could be alone for prayer. While they wait for their Teacher to return, the dusty-robed men warm themselves around a crackling fire. Relaxing after their long, tiring day, the disciples reminisce over the miracles they had seen the Master perform.

Finally, Jesus rejoins His followers. He listens for a moment to their conversation. Then with piercing gaze, He asks them a simple question, "Who do people say that I am?"

The disciples reply, "Some of them think you are John the Baptist. Others say you are Elijah or some other ancient prophet come back to life again."

Then Jesus responds quietly, "Who do you say I am?"

And Peter replies confidently, "The Christ of God."

If Jesus were to ask you, "Who do you say I am?" what would your answer be? Your response to this question will determine your eternal destiny—and the quality of life you can experience on this earth.

Considering the Evidence

I have yet to meet a person who has honestly considered the overwhelming evidence proving the deity of Jesus of Nazareth who does not admit that He is the Son of God. Yes, I have met some who do not believe that Jesus is the Son of God. But as we have talked and reasoned together, they have been honest in confessing, "I have not taken the time to read the Bible or to consider the historical facts concerning Jesus."

Their rejection and sometimes resentment of Christ has inevitably been based upon a lack of knowledge, an unfortunate emotional experience, upon the inconsistency of some Christian, or perhaps upon the influence of a high school teacher or college professor; but always they have admitted that they have not honestly considered the person of Jesus Christ and His claims on their lives.

Some years ago, I was speaking to a group of students at the University of California in Los Angeles. Immediately following my address,

an angry young student whom I later discovered was the leader of a radical group on
campus approached me.

"I resent your effort to convince these
students to become Christians," he said. "You
have no right to impose your views on them.
You are older and more mature than they are,
and they are like putty in your hands. I object
to your trying to convert them into becoming
Christians."

Of course, he had conveniently failed to
acknowledge that his goal as leader of the
radical group on campus was to do everything
he could to influence the students to follow
his way. But rather than argue, I invited him to
our home for dinner. He agreed to come.

It was an interesting and delightful eve-
ning. We had a pleasant chat. I found him to be
a personable young man, brilliant of mind and
articulate. We had a good time together.

After we finished our meal, I thought it
appropriate to talk to him about the Lord Jesus
Christ. So I reached over and picked up my
Bible. "I would like to read something to you
from the Bible," I told him.

He reacted strongly. "I don't believe the
Bible," he declared. "I don't want to hear
anything you read. I've read the Bible from
cover to cover, and it's filled with contradic-
tions and myths. I don't believe a word of it!"

I responded calmly. "If you don't mind, I'll read a few portions anyway."

So I turned to the first chapter of the Gospel of John and read,

> *Before anything existed, there was Christ, with God. He has always been alive and is himself God...Eternal life is in him, and this life gives light to all mankind. His life is the light that shines through the darkness—and the darkness can never extinguish it.*

I read several more verses and finished with,

> *Christ became a human being and lived here on earth among us and was full of loving forgiveness and truth. And some of us have seen his glory—the glory of the only Son of the heavenly Father (John 1:1-14, TLB).*

"Let me see that," the young man said eagerly. "I don't think I've ever noticed that. I don't remember reading it." He went over the passage thoughtfully and handed the Bible back to me without comment.

Then I turned to Colossians 1, beginning with the 13th verse, and read,

> *[God] has rescued us out of the*

darkness and gloom of Satan's kingdom and brought us into the kingdom of his dear Son, who bought our freedom with his blood and forgave us all our sins.

Christ is the exact likeness of the unseen God. He existed before God made anything at all, and, in fact, Christ himself is the Creator who made everything in heaven and earth, the things we can see and the things we can't...all were made by Christ for his own use and glory. He was before all else began and it is his power that holds everything together.

It was through what his Son did that God cleared a path for everything to come to him—all things in heaven and on earth—for Christ's death on the cross has made peace with God for all by his blood (TLB).

Again he asked if he could read the passage for himself. He appeared to read the verses over and over again because some time passed before he returned the Bible to me.

Then I turned to Hebrews 1 and read verses 1 through 3.

Long ago God spoke in many different ways to our fathers through the prophets...telling them little by little about his plans.

But now in these days he has spoken to us through his Son to whom he has given everything, and through whom he made the world and everything there is.

God's Son shines out with God's glory, and all that God's Son is and does marks him as God. He regulates the universe by the mighty power of his command. He is the one who died to cleanse us and clear our record of all sin, and then sat down in highest honor beside the great God of heaven (TLB).

By this time, the young man was obviously moved. His whole attitude of belligerence and antagonism was gone. So I turned to 1 John 2:22,23 and read,

Who is the greatest liar? The one who says that Jesus is not Christ. Such a person is antichrist, for he does not believe in God the Father and in his Son. For a person who doesn't believe in Christ, God's Son, can't have God the Father either. But he who has Christ, God's Son, has God the Father also (TLB).

When I finished reading, we chatted briefly. After a while he stood and prepared to leave. I asked if he would write in our guest book. He nodded.

Following his name and address, he wrote these words, "The night of decision!" God's Holy Spirit had used the Word of God to break through his antagonism. Before my very eyes, the miracle had taken place. This young man had come face to face with the revolutionary, risen Son of God.

Your Invitation to Life

Have you discovered the joy and peace of personally placing your trust in Jesus Christ? Perhaps you have believed in the existence of God and His Son and have tried to live a good life but have never consciously invited Him to be your Savior and Lord.

No matter who you are—whether young or old, a professional or a student, married or single—at this very moment, you too can make the decision of a lifetime. Right now Jesus is knocking at the door of your heart. He offers you the same wonderful love and plan which hundreds of millions through the centuries have received with life-changing results. He has already paid the penalty for your sin. He is asking you, in the quiet of your heart, to yield your all to Him—your intellect, your will, your emotions.

Here are four spiritual laws or principles that will help you discover how to know God personally and experience the abundant life He promises.*

1. *God **LOVES** you and offers a wonderful **PLAN** for your life.*

God's Love

God so loved the world, that He gave His only begotten Son, that whoever believes in Him should not perish, but have eternal life (John 3:16, NASB).

God's Plan

(Christ speaking): I came that they might have life, and might have it abundantly [that it might be full and meaningful] (John 10:10, NASB).

Why is it that most people are not experiencing the abundant life? Because:

2. *Man is **SINFUL** and **SEPARATED** from God, so we cannot know Him personally or experience His love.*

---

*Adapted from my *Four Spiritual Laws* boklet.

Man is Sinful

For all have sinned and fall short of the glory of God (Romans 3:23, NASB).

We were all created to have fellowship with God, but because of our stubborn self-will, we chose to go our own independent way and fellowship with God was broken. This self-will, characterized by an attitude of active rebellion or passive indifference, is evidence of what the Bible calls sin.

Man is Separated

The wages of sin is death [spiritual separation from God] (Romans 6:23).

God is holy and man is sinful. A great gulf separates us from God because He cannot tolerate sin. People often try to achieve the abundant life through their own efforts, such as living a good life or devotion to philosophy or religion. But the Bible clearly teaches that there is only one way to bridge this gulf:

3. *Jesus Christ is God's **ONLY** provision for our sin. Through Him you can know and*

experience God's love and plan for your life.

God's Word records three important facts to verify this principle:

Jesus Died in Our Place

God demonstrated His own love toward us, in that while we were yet sinners, Christ died for us (Romans 5:8).

Jesus Rose From the Dead

Christ died for our sins...He was buried...He was raised on the third day according to the Scriptures...He appeared to Cephas [Peter], then to the twelve. After that He appeared to more than five hundred (1 Corinthians 15:3-6, NASB).

Jesus Is the Only Way to God

Jesus said to him, "I am the way, and the truth, and the life; no one comes to the Father, but through Me" (John 14:6, NASB).

Thus, God has taken the loving initiative to bridge the gulf which separates us from Him by sending His Son, Jesus

Christ, to die on the cross in our place to pay the penalty for our sin. But it is not enough just to know these truths...

4. *We must individually* **RECEIVE** *Jesus Christ as Savior and Lord; then we can know and experience God's plan for our lives.*

We Must Receive Christ

As many as received Him, to them He gave the right to become children of God, even to those who believe in His name (John 1:12, NASB).

We Receive Christ by Personal Invitation

(Christ is speaking): Behold, I stand at the door and knock; if anyone hears My voice and opens the door, I will come in to him (Revelation 3:20, NASB).

Thus, receiving Christ involves turning to God from self (repentance) and trusting Christ to come into our lives to forgive our sins and to make us the kind of people He wants us to be. Just to agree intellectually that Jesus Christ is the Son of God and that He died on the cross for our sins is not enough. Nor is it enough to have an emotional experience. We receive Jesus Christ by faith, as an act of the will.

These two circles represent two kinds of lives:

SELF-DIRECTED LIFE

S—Self is on the throne

†—Christ is outside the life

●—Interests are directed by self, often resulting in discord and frustration

CHRIST-DIRECTED LIFE

†— Christ is in the life and on the throne

S— Self is yielding to Christ

●—Interests are directed by Christ, resulting in harmony with God's plan

Which circle best represents your life?

Which circle would you like to have represent your life?

You can receive Jesus Christ right now by faith through prayer. God knows your heart and is not so concerned with your words as He is with the attitude of your heart. Here is a suggested prayer which has helped millions of men and women around the world express faith in Him and invite Him into their lives:

> *Lord Jesus, I want to know You personally. Thank You for dying on the cross for my sins. I open the door of my life and receive You as my Savior and Lord. Thank You for forgiving my sins and giving me eternal life. Take control of the throne of my life. Make me the kind of person you want me to be.*

Experiencing the Life

If you truly believe that Jesus Christ is the Son of God, that He died on the cross for your sins and was raised from the dead, and if you prayed this prayer sincerely from your heart, you have just received the Lord Jesus Christ as your personal Savior and Lord. You are now a child of God. Today you have begun to experience God's wonderful love and forgiveness.

By receiving Christ as Savior and Lord you are assured of everlasting life with Him in heaven:

> *He who has the Son has life; he who does not have the Son of God does not have the life. These things I have written to you who believe in the name of the Son of God, in order that you might know that you have eternal life (1 John 5:12,13, NASB).*

So, in summary, when you received Christ by faith, as an act of your will, many wonderful things happened including the following:

1. Christ came into your life (Revelation 3:20; Colossians 1:27).

2. Your sins were forgiven (Colossians 1:14).

3. You became a child of God (John 1:12).

4. You received eternal life (John 5:24).

5. You began the great adventure for which God created you (John 10:10; 2 Corinthians 5:17; 1 Thessalonians 5:18).

Can you think of anything more wonderful that could happen to you than receiving Christ? Take a moment right now to thank God in prayer for what He has done for you. By thanking Him, you demonstrate your faith. Ephesians 2:8,9 reminds us that we do not earn God's love and forgiveness by our good works. Salvation is a gift from God which we receive by faith.

Once we have received Christ as Savior, we do not need to invite Him in again.* He promises His followers, "I am with you always,

---

* To learn more about how you can be sure you are a Christian, see Appendix A.

even to the end of the world" (Matthew 28:20, TLB). His Holy Spirit will dwell within us for the remainder of our lives.[61]

Now that you have become a child of God, you will discover that the claims of history's greatest revolutionary are true for you today. To help you grow in your new life in Christ, I have listed resources at the end of this booklet that will help strengthen your walk with the Lord. I encourage you to study His Word, the Bible, and obey His commands. Go to Him daily in prayer, trusting Him for every detail of your life. As you do so, you will experience the abundant life He has promised. And as you faithfully worship and serve in a local church, you too will know the love and fellowship of other believers, the body of Christ. These principle have been used by God to enrich my life since I became a Christian in 1945.

Paul was so thrilled about Jesus that he exclaimed in Colossians 1:28, "Everywhere we go we talk about Christ to all who will listen" (TLB). I encourage you to experience the joy of helping others discover this exciting life for themselves as well. Share your faith in Christ with your friends, loved ones, and neighbors at every opportunity. Take the initiative to tell everyone you meet about the person and claims of our Lord Jesus Christ and the revolutionary way He can change their lives. This practice has been especially meaningful to me.

You, too, can be a part of the wonderful adventure of spreading His words and teachings everywhere you go throughout the world through your prayers, your finances, and your personal involvement. You can help others discover the true destiny for which they were created by introducing them to the Man who has no equal.

Self-Study Guide

1. Why is Jesus Christ considered history's "greatest revolutionary?" (See pp. 14-17)

    _____

    _____

2. Why is Jesus Christ more than a prophet?

    _____

    _____

3. What qualities make Jesus a great teacher? (See pp. 29-33)

    _____

    _____

4. Could Jesus have orchestrated the events of His life to fulfill the prophecies of the Old Testament concerning the Messiah? Why? (See pp. 40-46)

    _____

    _____

    _____

5. In what ways has Jesus changed the world? (See pp. 79-89) How has He influenced life in your community?

    _____

    _____

6. What did Jesus claim about Himself in the following passages? Why does this make Him unique?
   a. John 10:30   b. Luke 24:44   c. John 11:25

   _____

   _____

   _____

7. What were some consequences of the fall of man? (See pp. 57-60)

   _____

   _____

   _____

8. What was the purpose of the death of Christ? (See pp. 60-62)

   _____

   _____

   _____

9. What does the resurrection prove about Jesus Christ? (See pp. 73-75)

   _____

   _____

10. Why is the ascension of Christ necessary for our redemption? (See pp. 76,77)

    _____

    _____

    _____

11. What was your view of Jesus before reading this booklet? What do you believe now?

_____

_____

_____

12. List five people in your circle of influence (family, friends or neighbors) who do not know Christ personally and pray for each one by name. Ask God to give you an opportunity to share His love and forgiveness through Jesus Christ with them.

_____

_____

_____

_____

_____

Group Discussion Questions

1. How has the influence of Jesus changed your country? Your neighborhood? Your family? Your life?

2. How did the changed lives of the disciples prove that Jesus is who He said He was? How can a changed life today give witness to the validity of Christ's claims?

3. How did the unique birth and life of Jesus prepare the way for our redemption? What has He asked us to do in response to His great love?

4. The resurrection of Jesus ranks as history's most revolutionary event. How does it prove Christ's claim to be God? Why is the resurrection so essential to our faith?

5. Would you like to live in a community where the message and influence of Jesus of Nazareth have not been felt? Why?

6. Break into groups of two or three and discuss a strategy to reach individuals in your circle of influence (family, friends or neighbors) with the Good News of God's love and forgiveness through Jesus Christ.

Appendix A

You Can Be Sure
You Are a Christian

If you have received Christ, sometimes you may wonder if you really are a Christian. You may say, "I believe Jesus Christ is the Son of God and died for my sins. Yet I don't feel like a child of God."

How, then, can you be sure that you are a Christian? Is there some kind of confirmation that God gives to those who sincerely receive Christ? I believe there is a three-fold confirmation that Jesus Christ is in our lives.

1. External Witness of God's Word

The promise of God's Word, not your feelings, is your authority. His Word is totally reliable. As a Christian, you are to live by faith in the trustworthiness of God and His holy, inspired Word.

First John 5:11,12 confirm that Christ is in your life if you received Him:

> *This is the testimony: God has given us eternal life, and this life is in his Son. He who has the Son has life, he who does not have the Son of God does not have life.*

John 1:12,13 echo this promise:

> *To all who received him, to those who*
> *believe in his name, he gave the right to*
> *become children of God—children born*
> *not of natural descent, nor of human*
> *decision or a husband's will, but born of*
> *God.*

A doctor and his wife from Zurich, Switzerland, sent their son to the University of California, Los Angeles, to complete his doctoral studies in meteorology. Their son Hans received Christ at one of our meetings and wrote to his parents about his new-found faith. He mentioned my name as the one who had introduced him to our Lord. They wrote back asking if he would set up an appointment for them to see me. At great expense the father and mother flew all the way from Zurich to Los Angeles for the express purpose of becoming Christians.

It was a dramatic moment for me when this man of great influence and means, with his wife, came into my office near the UCLA campus. He began our meeting by explaining his own spiritual journey. "I was an atheist for years," he said, "but I found no future in atheism. So, I began to study the religions of the Orient. Again, there was no satisfaction. Then, someone told me the New Testament was where I would find my answers. I began to read it and became convinced Jesus was the one I was looking for. Then we received the letter from Hans telling us how you had helped him to become a Christian. We want you to tell us what you told Hans."

Well, you can imagine how I felt! What a privilege it was to talk to this wonderful couple about our Savior, the living Christ.

I explained how they could receive Christ by simply inviting Him into their lives. He interrupted me. "Mr. Bright," he said, "I've already done that. I receive Jesus into my life every day. On some occasions I ask Him in several times a day."

Now I was puzzled. Relatively new in leading people to the Lord in those days, I didn't know what to say. I prayed silently, "God, help me. What do I say now?"

Ephesians 2:8,9 flashed on the screen of my mind:

> *It is by grace you have been saved; through faith—and this not from yourselves, it is the gift of God—not by works, so that no one can boast.*

I explained that it is not enough to ask Jesus into your life; you must believe He will come in as He promised. "God honors faith," I said. "He does not honor your invitation to Him to come in. It is your faith in Him and His promise that, if you open the door, He will come in[62] that He honors. You can ask Jesus into your life a thousand times, and He will never come unless you believe, on the basis of His promise, that He will come. You can depend upon Him to keep His promise to come in if you ask Him as an expression of faith."

I suggested that they invite Christ into their lives on the basis of God's promise. Even before we prayed, the father's face lit up with assurance of his salvation, and he began to laugh.

He turned to his dear wife and spoke to her in German, telling her what I had shared with him. She began to laugh, a holy laugh, a laugh of assurance. They had been looking for God, and now the light went on, and they were filled with joy.

I was telling that story later to a gathering of thousands of people at one of our training conferences. A woman came up to me afterward. She was in her eighties, her hair was snow white, and her radiant face was stained with tears.

"I've been a Sunday school teacher for more than forty years," she said. "Every day of my life, I have asked Jesus into my life, and I've never been sure He was there. Tonight, by faith, I asked Him in for the last time as you told the story of the man from Switzerland. Now I know He is there because He said He would come in. He promised never to leave me nor forsake me.[63] I'm never going to insult Him by asking Him in again. For the rest of my life, as an expression of faith, I'm going to begin every day thanking Jesus that He is with me as He promised."

2. Internal Witness of the Holy Spirit

The apostle Paul writes, "The Spirit himself testifies with our spirit that we are God's children" (Romans 8:16). Paul emphasized the validity of this inner source of assurance to the Thessalonian Christians:

> *When we brought you the good news,*
> *it was not just meaningless chatter to you;*
> *no, you listened with great interest. What*
> *we told you produced a powerful effect on*
> *you, for the Holy Spirit gave you great*
> *and full assurance that what we said was*
> *true (1 Thessalonians 1:5, TLB).*

3. Changed Life

Your changed life is a witness to the fact that you are a Christian. Paul records, "When someone becomes a Christian he becomes a brand new person inside. He is not the same anymore. A new life has begun!" (2 Corinthians 5:17). John says:

> *How can we be sure that we belong to*
> *him? By looking within ourselves: are we*
> *really trying to do what he wants us to?*
> *Someone may say, "I am a Christian; I*
> *belong to Christ." But if he doesn't do*
> *what Christ tells him to do, he is a liar. But*
> *those who do what Christ tells them to*
> *will learn to love God more and more. This*
> *is the way to know whether or not you are*
> *a Christian. Anyone who says he is a*
> *Christian should live as Christ did (1 John*
> *2:3-6, TLB).*

If you have invited Jesus Christ into your life, you can now have confidence that He is in your life and has given you eternal life as He promised. Jesus would not deceive you. You can be sure, if you asked Him into your life, He now lives within you and will give you the abundant life He promised.

Remember His promise, "I will never leave you nor forsake you" (Hebrews 13:5, NKJ).

Appendix B
The "JESUS" Film in the Commonwealth of Independent States

The "JESUS" film, sponsored and financed by Campus Crusade for Christ, is now being shown to many millions of people in theaters and public schools throughout the Commonwealth of Independent States in the various languages of the republics. At each showing, the Gospel of Luke containing *Who Is Jesus* and the *Four Spiritual Laws* is given to each one who attends.

The film ends with an invitation to receive Jesus Christ as Savior and Lord, and the booklet concludes with a decision page which encourages the viewers to record their decision and other responses.

These comment sheets are then placed in the hands of local pastors who are trained to follow up the expressed desires of the responders.

We are prayerfully anticipating that tens of millions will receive Jesus as their Savior and Lord while viewing the film "JESUS" in the theaters and schools of the Commonwealth of Independent States.

The showing of the "JESUS" film is part of an international strategy called New Life 2000 which is designed to establish 6,000 New Life Training Teams and 12,000 "JESUS" film teams throughout the world.

Source Notes

1. Luke 12:1.
2. Philip Schaff, *The Person of Christ* (New York: American Tract Society, 1913), p. 33. *The World Christian Encyclopedia*, edited by David Barrett, estimates the world's Christian population at 32.4 percent in 1985.
3. Matthew 16:13-15; Mark 8:27-30; Luke 9:18-20.
4. Mark 5:42; 9:18; Luke 7:11; 8:41.
5. Matthew 9:32; 12:22; Mark 1:26; Luke 4:35.
6. Matthew 9:20; Mark 5:22; Luke 8:43.
7. Matthew 14:15; Mark 6:41; Luke 9:12; John 6:5.
8. Mark 8:27 (NASB).
9. Mark 8:28 (TLB).
10. Philip Schaff, *The Person of Christ* (New York: George H. Doran Company, 1913), pp. 137,138.
11. Schaff, *The Person of Christ*, pp. 137,138.
12. Matthew. 14:1-12.
13. Matthew 26:65,66.
14. Sherwood Eliot Wirt and Kersten Beckstrom, *Living Quotations for Christians* (New York: Harper & Row, Publishers, 1974), number 1807.
15. Charles Malik, *Christ and Crisis* (Grand Rapids: William B. Eerdmans Publishing Company, 1962), pp. 67,68,70.
16. John Eldredge and Tom Hess, "Pro-life Heroes in a Hostile Age," *Citizen*, May 21, 1990, p. 11.
17. Alexander Roberts and James Donaldson, eds., *The Ante-Nicene Fathers* (Grand Rapids: William B. Eerdmans Publishing Co., 1973), p. 46.
18. John F. Walvoord, *Jesus Christ Our Lord* (Chicago: Moody Press, 1969), p. 22.
19. Michael Horton, ed., *The Agony of Deceit* (Chicago:Moody Press, 1990), p. 98.

20. Matthew 4:23-25; Luke 13:10.
21. John 14:24.
22. John 3:16-19; 12:46-48; 15:16.
23. Mark 7:6-23; Matthew 20:28; John 3:16-18.
24. John 19:38-42; (100 litras [12 oz each] of spices).
25. Josephus, *The Works of Josephus* (Peabody, MA: Hendrickson Publishers, 1987), p. 480.
26. Merle D'Aubigne', D.D., *History of the Reformation* (Grand Rapids: Baker Book House, 1976), p. 42.
27. Frank S. Mead, ed., *The Encyclopedia of Religious Quotations* (Old Tappan, NJ: Fleming H. Revell Company, 1976), p. 90.
28. John Bartlett, *Familiar Quotations* (Boston: Little, Brown and Company, 1955), p. 618.
29. Mead, *Encyclopedia*, pp. 92,93.
30. C.S. Lewis, *Surprised by Joy: The Shape of My Early Life* (New York: Harcourt and Brace, 1966), pp. 228,229.
31. C.S. Lewis, *Mere Christianity* (New York: The MacMillan Company, 1960), pp. 40,41.
32. Peter W. Stoner and Robert C. Newman, *Science Speaks* (Chicago: Moody Press, 1976), pp. 106-112.
33. Herbert Lockyer, *All the Messianic Prophecies of the Bible* (Grand Rapids: Zondervan Publishing House, 1973), p. 64.
34. Psalm 22:18; fulfillment in John 19:24.
35. Matthew 7:28,29; 22:15-46.
36. Mark 1:10,11.
37. Luke 4:40-43; 8:40-48.
38. Mark 2:14-18; 10:13-16.
39. John 17; Luke 22:40-46.
40. Romans 5:1,2; 5:8-10.
41. Matthew 8:2.
42. John 9:35-39.
43. Matthew 14:33.

44. John 11:23-25.
45. Adapted from Genesis 1 and 2.
46. Genesis 3.
47. Genesis 3:16-19,22-24.
48. Genesis 3:1-19; Romans 5:12; John 3:19.
49. John 5:42; Romans 8:7; 7:18,23,24.
50. Ephesians 1:3-14.
51. John 1:1-4,10-14; 3:16,17; 8:46; 1 Peter 2:21,22;
    Hebrews 4:15; Isaiah 53:5,6; 1 Corinthians 15:3;
    2 Corinthians 5:21; 1 Peter 2:24; 3:18; Mark 10:45;
    Hebrews 2:9; Romans 5:6-21.
52. Herbert Lockyer, *All the Doctrines of the Bible*
    (Grand Rapids: Zondervan Publishing House,
    1964), p. 40.
53. Philippians 2:6-11; John 1:1-14; Romans 1:2-5,
    9:5; 1 Timothy 3:16; Hebrews 2:14; 1 John 1:1-3.
54. Hebrews 4:15.
55. Finis Jennings Dake, *God's Plan for Man*
    (Lawrenceville, GA: Dake Bible Sales, Inc., 1949),
    pp. 372,373.
56. Matthew 28:1-10.
57. Luke 24:13-32.
58. 1 Corinthians 15:3-6.
59. Acts 1:8.
60. Wirt and Beckstrom, *Living Quotations*, No.
    1749.
61. 2 Corinthians 1:22.
62. Revelations 3:20.
63. Hebrews 13:5.

Resources to Help You Grow and Share the Good News

Transferable Concepts to help you experience and share the abundant Christian life. Bill Bright.

*How You Can Experience God's Love
    and Forgiveness*
How You Can Be Filled With the Holy Spirit
How You Can Walk in the Spirit
How You Can Be a Fruitful Witness
How You Can Introduce Others to Christ
*How You Can Help Fulfill the
    Great Commission*
How You Can Love By Faith
How You Can Pray With Confidence
*How You Can Experience the Adventure
    of Giving*

Life Without Equal: Discover Purpose, Peace and Power for Living. Bill Bright. A presentation of the length and breadth of the Christian's freedom in Jesus Christ and how believers can release Christ's resurrection power for life and ministry.

Witnessing Without Fear. Bill Bright, with foreword by Billy Graham. A step-by-step guide to sharing your faith with confidence. Ideal for both individual and group study; a Gold Medallion Award winner.

Come Help Change the World. Bill Bright. A stirring call to participate in the greatest adventure the human spirit can know: fulfilling the Great Commission.

Have You Heard of the Four Spiritual Laws? Bill Bright. One of the most effective evangelistic tools ever developed, the *Four Spiritual Laws* provide an easy-to-use way of sharing your faith with others. An estimated 1.5 billion copies have been distributed worldwide.

Would You Like to Know God Personally? Bill Bright. A new adaptation of the *Four Spiritual Laws*, presented as four principles for establishing a personal relationship with God through faith in Jesus Christ.

Have You Made the Wonderful Discovery of the Spirit-filled Life? Bill Bright. Discover the reality of the Spirit-filled life and how to live in moment-by-moment dependence on Him.

The Holy Spirit: Key to Supernatural Living. Bill Bright. This book helps you enter into the Spirit-filled life and shares how you can experience a life of supernatural power and victory.

The Secret. Bill Bright. An inspiring book showing you how to discover a new dimension of happiness and joy in your Christian walk and draw upon the purpose, power and guidance of the Holy Spirit.

Promises: A Daily Guide to Supernatural Living. Bill Bright. A daily devotional guide to help you live a supernatural life every day by meditating and acting upon God's promises.

Reaching Your World. Bill Bright. Training in how to introduce others to Christ. Six-part video/workbook package for congregational meetings,

Sunday school, midweek Bible studies, and evangelism training. Includes student workbooks, leader's guide, copies of Witnessing Without Fear and evangelistic booklets.

A Man Without Equal (video). Bill Bright. This 30-minute video shows how Jesus was the most unique person who ever lived and illustrates how He changes the way we live and think today. Excellent for Sunday school, group meetings, or personal study.

Ten Basic Steps. Bill Bright. A comprehensive curriculum for the Christian who wants to master the basics of Christian growth. Used by hundreds of thousands worldwide. Student and teacher's manuals available.

Introduction — Uniqueness of Jesus
Step 1   — The Christian Adventure
Step 2   — The Christian and the Abundant Life
Step 3   — The Christian and the Holy Spirit
Step 4   — The Christian and Prayer
Step 5   — The Christian and the Bible
Step 6   — The Christian and Obedience
Step 7   — The Christian and Witnessing
Step 8   — The Christian and Stewardship
Step 9   — Highlights of the Old Testament
Step 10   — Highlights of the New Testament

Books by Bill and Vonette Bright

Managing Stress in Marriage: Help for Couples on the Fast Track. Bill and Vonette Bright. Practical help for couples facing life in the fast lane. Learn to deal with stress through looking at the Brights' experiences with two careers, ministry obligations and life changes. Winner of 1991 Silver Angel Award.

The Greatest Lesson I've Ever Learned (men). Bill Bright, editor. Fascinating personal glimpses into the lives of 39 prominent Christian men including Charles Colson, Billy Graham, James Dobson, Tony Campolo and Luis Palau.

The Greatest Lesson I've Ever Learned (women). Vonette Bright, editor. More than 20 prominent Christian women share the lessons that shaped their lives. Features Barbara Bush, Ann Kiemel Anderson, Joni Eareckson Tada, and more! Winner of 1991 Silver Angel Award.

BILL BRIGHT is founder and president of Campus Crusade for Christ, International. The ministry serves in 136 major countries representing 97 percent of the world's population. Dr. Bright and his dedicated associates of more than 30,000 full-time staff and trained volunteers have introduced tens of millions of people to Jesus Christ, discipling millions to live Spirit-filled, fruitful lives of purpose and power for the glory of God.

Dr. Bright did graduate studies at Princeton and Fuller Theological seminaries from 1946 to 1951. The recipient of many national and international awards, including five honorary doctorates and International Churchman of the Year, he is the author of numerous books and publications committed to helping fulfill the Great Commission. His special focus is New Life 2000, an international effort to help reach more than six billion people with the gospel of our Lord Jesus Christ and help fulfill the Great Commission by the year 2000.

Response Form

☐ Please send me more information on how I can become a Christian.

☐ I have just received Jesus Christ as my Savior and Lord and would appreciate more information on how to experience the abundant Christian life.

☐ Please inform me of other materials for Christian growth.

Name _____

Address _____

City _____

State _____ Zip _____

Phone (____) _____

Please check the appropriate box or boxes and mail this form in an envelope to:

Bill Bright
Campus Crusade for Christ
Sunport Center
100 Sunport Lane
Orlando, FL 32809